To Bodi

The Author

Barney Norris was born in Sussex in 1987. Upon leaving university he founded Up In Arms theatre company with the director Alice Hamilton. His plays include *Visitors* (Up In Arms, Arcola Theatre and tour), *Fear Of Music* (Up In Arms/Out of Joint, tour) and *At First Sight* (Up In Arms, tour and Latitude Festival). This is his first book.

To Bodies Gone

The Theatre of Peter Gill

Barney Norris

SEREN

Seren is the book imprint of
Poetry Wales Press Ltd
Nolton Street, Bridgend, Wales

www.serenbooks.com
facebook.com/SerenBooks
Twitter: @SerenBooks

ISBN 978-1-78172-181-0
Epub 978-1-78172-182-7
Mobi 978-1-78172-183-4

A CIP record for this title is available from the British Library

The publisher works with the financial assistance
of the Welsh Books Council

Cover photograph: a scene from *The Sleepers Den*,
© Victoria and Albert Museum, London

Printed by Bell & Bain Ltd, Glasgow

CONTENTS

ACKNOWLEDGMENTS

For Peter.

With thanks to everyone who has supported the development of this project, particularly Alice, who introduced me to Peter's work; Bernard O'Donoghue and Sophie Ratcliffe, great teachers; Lindsay and Ivan, who made it possible for me to work with Peter; John Burgess, Graham Cowley, Kenneth Cranham, Terry Davies, William Gaskill, Michael Grandage, James Knowlson, John McGrath, Josie Rourke, Max Stafford-Clark, Stephen Unwin, Nicholas Wright, Dinah Wood and all at Casarotto Ramsay; Mick Felton and Seren; Panda, Bella and Charlie; and to Peter Lawlor and Dad, conversationalists whose examples animate this writing.

Yesterday is not a milestone that has been passed, but a daystone on the beaten track of the years, and immediately part of us, within us, heavy and dangerous.

Samuel Beckett, Proust

PROLOGUE

There can be few bodies of work that are more rewarding when read continuously than the plays of Peter Gill. From the beginning of his career, Gill's theatre has been engaged in a Van Gogh-like search, not quite to find the beauty in a pair of old boots, but rather to reveal a beauty that is always present in anything, weathered or leather or otherwise. This hard stare at the ordinary world, his extraordinary way of seeing, connects each new play to the last like beads on a rosary. To read Gill's plays chronologically is to witness the expansion of both a mind and a world, beautiful and distinctive, made richer and more compelling with each new statement. This book is a study of Gill's work, the first volume to address the entirety of his career to date, and an opportunity to engage with this haunting and beautiful writer in unprecedented depth. Whether readers are new to the work, or admirers of long standing, I hope it will shed light.

That Gill's plays stand as a major achievement of the contemporary theatre is one reason for this study. However, such is the nature of his work in the theatre that if he had never written a line in his life, he would still be a vital subject for critical attention. His parallel careers as a director and, particularly through his work at the National Theatre Studio, as a supporter and nurturer of new voices and ideas, have made him one of the most influential and admired theatre artists of the last fifty years. Since making his name at the Royal Court in the 1960s, he has directed more than 100 productions at the Court, Riverside Studios, the National Theatre and on numerous other stages in Britain and around the world. His achievements mark him out as an artist of singular vision, whose poetic naturalism and fierce humanism have been lighting up the theatre ever since, as a key figure at the Royal

Court in the years after George Devine launched the English Stage Company, he helped position it at the heart of our culture. My study will therefore engage with Gill's work as a director as well as with his writing – with the whole of his creative life.

★

Peter Gill was born into a Catholic family in Cardiff in 1939 to George and Margaret Gill, and attended St Illtyd's Grammar School in the city. It was during these early years of his life that much of the imaginative landscape of his drama was first mapped out – a great deal of his writing returns to the Cardiff of his childhood, exploring the vanished world of his youth, traversing through his work the distance placed between himself and his past by geography and time. On leaving school, Gill moved to London to become first a stage manager, and then an actor. He had a short and busy career on stage and screen, working for the Royal Shakespeare Company and appearing, among other things, in the film *Zulu*, but by the mid 1960s he had begun to turn to directing – a transition he documents in his memoir *Apprenticeship*. He became an assistant director at the Royal Court in 1964, and directed his first productions there, single performances presented without decor on the stage of other Royal Court productions on Sunday nights, before achieving success with his productions of the plays of D.H. Lawrence. He continued to work at the Royal Court, in Europe and in North America until 1976, when he became the founding Artistic Director of Riverside Studios, which, under his leadership, became one of the leading arts centres in Europe. In 1980 he became an Associate Director of the National Theatre – a position he held until 1997 – and in 1984 he founded the National Theatre Studio, which he ran until 1990. Since 1997 he has continued to work at the Royal Court and the National Theatre, as well as with the RSC, the other company with whom he has maintained a relationship throughout his career, as well as working regularly at the Donmar Warehouse, the Almeida Theatre and the Peter Hall Company at the Theatre Royal Bath, among others. A complete index of his theatre career can be found at the back of this book.

Gill is first of all a social realist, whose work depicts the conditions of human lives around him and contains in those depictions implicit broader observations of the societies which impose and maintain those conditions on their citizens. Time and again, his productions have been seen to afford extraordinary focus and attention to the supporting casts of plays – servants, peasants, and all who use the back stairs. This emphasis on ordinary people is at the heart of his work, and its distinguishing quality is an ability to imbue those characters, so often overlooked in history books but caught here and there in art, with a dignity that makes their endurance of the limits of their lives numinous and heroic. Gill takes the ordinary and makes it extraordinary. In his own writing, however, Gill complicates this aesthetic – while his plays are written with minute, intensely naturalistic attention to detail at the level of the individual line or scene, they are structurally complex, often radical in their form. They could not be adequately described as realist work, and an analysis of those structures is at the heart of this book.

Gill's work as a director spans the canon of English language theatre, ranging from Shakespeare, Otway, Webster and Middleton and Rowley to major contemporary figures such as Joe Orton, Harold Pinter, John Osborne and Nicholas Wright, via Wilde, Shaw and Granville Barker. Like many of his contemporaries, he is popularly associated with the work of one particular writer (as Max Stafford-Clark is with Caryl Churchill or Stella Feehily, Richard Eyre with David Hare, or William Gaskill with Edward Bond). Unlike his contemporaries, however, the writer Gill is most closely associated with is himself: since his first play, *The Sleepers Den*, he has directed the first productions of almost all his work. In this, he recalls Samuel Beckett, who directed the first productions of the majority of his dramatic output, although Beckett never pursued a career as a director beyond the staging of his own plays. Besides his own work, the writers Gill has directed most regularly are Shakespeare, Lawrence, Chekhov and Osborne.

Summarising the salient facts of a life is always difficult. What may look like great events from a distance might not seem half as important to the subject as certain afternoons we might never notice if he didn't draw them to our attention. But while this is not a biography of Peter Gill, it is undoubtedly necessary at the outset of this study to set out some of the details of his life. Gill's background is unconventional in the context of his theatrical peers – he never went to university, his father worked as a docker and a warehouseman, and he came from a city that has given up its theatrical secrets warily (Gill is to date the only Welsh writer besides Dylan Thomas to have been staged at the National Theatre, although the work of National Theatre Wales seems sure to change that before long, as a new generation of Welsh playwrights emerges). Not only does this mark him out as an unusual figure among a generation of directors dominated by university graduates and members of the middle class; it is also of direct bearing on a study of his work. Gill has made his life into the fabric of his theatre. His plays read as a response to experience, a way of addressing and collecting life in order to question it and love it as it passes. Throughout the plays, ideas are tied to the places and experiences of his childhood, his adult life in London, and above all to a sense of exile from his background and displacement from the world around him, and so reference to this context, his surrounding world, is highly beneficial for a reading of the work.

The extent to which Gill himself would agree with such a biographical reading is open to question. Throughout his work, influence and motivation are revealing when unearthed, but diffi-cult to ascribe. He has stated that quotations and references in his plays are frequently unintentional – while he is aware Marcel Proust is quoted in *Small Change*, for example, he denies knowing at the time he wrote them that both *Small Change* and *The Sleepers Den* drew their titles from the poetry of John Donne. In this he recalls the critical writings of the poet and editor Don Paterson, who suggests in *Reading Shakespeare's Sonnets* that the organisations of a poet tend to be subconscious (or Beckett again, who mischeviously claims in *Watt* that there are 'no symbols where none intended' in his own work). The difficulty of attributing influence or uncovering the underlying logical structures of the material of the plays is part of what makes Gill so fascinating to read. He is an instinctive writer, and influences in his work are the organisations of the preconscious mind, collecting the nebulous material of a subconscious into a statement. Gill himself has described his process of writing as a slow clotting of ideas, words and sequences over years into a story. His ability to let that story develop its own form in its own time, to let the subconscious do its own work rather than write to prefabricated, 'well-made' structures, is a key to the originality of his plays.

I have used the term 'parallel careers' to describe Gill's work as a writer and a director, but of course this is not quite accurate. The Peter Gill who wrote *Small Change* and *The York Realist* is the same man who directed the D.H. Lawrence plays or Robert Holman's *Making Noise Quietly*, who founded and ran Riverside Studios and the National Theatre Studio. These are different facets of the same life, and it is my intention here to address them all, in order to attempt a comprehensive portrait of Gill's theatre. I hope I will encourage people to see and produce this work, to engage with this extraordinary writer and director. John Burgess, Gill's long-standing colleague and friend, has written that it 'sometimes seems as if Peter Gill's plays are one of the best kept secrets of the British theatre'. I have written this book because I think they ought to be among the worst kept. I think everyone should read them, and one intention of this book is to spread the word as best I can about these plays.

My other intention, which I imagine is always the first intention of any study of an artist's work, and which I hope readers will enjoy sharing with me, is to spend time immersed in Gill's theatre. As I began by saying, I believe there are few bodies of work that are more satisfying when read continuously than the plays of Peter Gill.

1. PHILOSOPHIES

Allow me to start with an anecdote.

In 2010, Gill directed the British premiere of a play called *The Aliens* by the American playwright Annie Baker at the Bush Theatre. The play, Baker's third, had been a success in its first production in New York, and the Bush secured a superb company to introduce her work to English audiences: Gill was joined by the designer Lucy Osborne, and the company consisted of Olly Alexander, Mackenzie Crook and Ralf Little.

I had first encountered Gill's work five years previously when I attended a school performance of *Small Change*. Two years later, while a student, I wanted to try directing, and resolved to have a go at *Small Change* myself. Feeling unequal to the challenges of the script, and hopeful of an opportunity to meet a real playwright – our theatre being largely obsessed with London, I hadn't had many opportunities to talk to writers while growing up in Wiltshire, because they very rarely visited – I wrote a letter to Gill, asking to interview him for a student magazine. He invited me to meet him at Theatre Royal Bath while he opened *The Importance Of Being Earnest* there, prior to its tour and West End season. I travelled down to Somerset and we met in the foyer of his hotel, where I listened to him talk for an hour, then got on the train home and realised I hadn't asked any of the questions I'd planned. I made up the article and wrote to him again, asking if we could meet and talk in more detail about *Small Change*.

This time we met at his flat in Hammersmith and I got round to asking Gill about his play. It was a memorable conversation. I was struck by the disparity between the complex structure of the work I was trying to direct and the pragmatic simplicity with which Gill discussed it. I was trying to understand the logic of its architecture. Gill's only advice was – 'do you know who Colin Jackson is? The hurdler. Get them to listen to him. If they say it like him you'll be all right. The trick is to get the long 'a' in Caardiff.'

What I was encountering was one of the abiding hallmarks of Gill's style – an understanding of the job as being in large part about the practical management of the stage. This practicality, I learned later, is always at the heart of Gill's engagement with the theatre, whether his own or other people's. In 2012 I directed a short play at the Lyric Hammersmith, which Gill came to see. I had worked out a staging before rehearsals began which I thought got round the two problems that needed solving in the production – the fact that the writer hadn't moved the characters much in the scene (a single exit and entrance for one, and anything else the other two did had to be superimposed, as the dialogue implied they were static), and the fact that the Lyric Hammersmith studio stage resembles a train platform. Setting a static office scene where everyone needed to be round one table on a stage wider than it was deep caused immediate aesthetic and practical sightline problems I needed to grapple with. I came up with a solution that afforded all but five seats out of one hundred and fifty a good view, and on the opening night sat in one of the five, in order to minimise the number of people who would find me out. Unfortunately, Gill sat down with me, and I tried to ignore the way he peered round the head of the person in front throughout the show to try and see my upstage character's face as the scene played out.

I hoped as we walked to the bar after the performance that he would engage with the deft way the writer had been able to access a big political story through a simple situation (it was a story about a disciplinary meeting in an ASDA in the north of England; I spent a problematic amount of time in rehearsals talking about Bentham's panopticon, and the way the structures of the capitalist system enslave us into self-regulation, which didn't help the company much but entertained me), but all Gill wanted to talk about was the blocking. 'Why did you do it like that? Did you not know how wide the stage was?' I tried to explain that I had indeed known how wide the stage was, but the best I'd been able to come up with was a table skewed off-centre to cheat the actors into

sight for all but five of my audience. Remorselessly, Gill replied –
'but why would a table be skewed off-centre in an office?'
Indicating the position of props and actors with his hands on one
of the tables in the Lyric bar, he gave me a lesson in stage geome-
try, picking up on everything I had known wasn't working but
had planned to get away with. His rigorously practical reading of
the scene saw immediately through the fact that I hadn't solved
the problems in the script at all.

Back in 2007, when I eventually directed my production of
Small Change, Gill came to see it, and after that we kept in
occasional contact. I would attend workshops or meetings, and
enjoyed finding excuses to talk to him on the phone (Gill is an
eloquent polemical speaker, articulate and possessed of an
idiosyncratic frame of reference dominated by the modern
theatre, the Bloomsbury Group, abstract and conceptual art and
contemporary politics). I wrote my BA thesis on him and D.H.
Lawrence, graduated, and worked for a year at Oxford
Playhouse. At the end of this year I got a call from the Bush
Theatre asking me to assist Gill on *The Aliens*.

The process was a revelation. Gill built rehearsals out of
simple components – we spent the first week reading poems that
could create a context for the work, either by writers the characters might have read – Bukowski – or that might serve to enrich
the tone of the production – Whitman. We read a scene from a
Restoration play to get a flavour of a radically different writing
style, where everything was written rather than implicated, in
order to focus in by stealth on the style we were to rehearse our
play in; we listened to extracts from Gill's diary, got to know each
other, and then, after finally reading the play on Thursday (by
which time the company attacked it with an extraordinary intensity and focus that perhaps came from keeping them away from
the text for a little while), we began to put it on its feet.

There is a certain amount of magic that happens in the
crucial rehearsal week when a play moves from table work to
being off book, which can't be adequately analysed in any study,
and which is where good directors earn their money. It's built up
out of minute and painstaking decisions and dealings with actors

that are apparently unremarkable as they happen, a series of small refinements that become, while no one is looking, the pattern and character of a production, as carefully calibrated through conversation, trial, error and hard work as any mechanical engine. This is the alchemical moment when plays are made. By the time the actors are off book, the nature of a production is established in their minds, and therefore also on the marked-up floor of the rehearsal space where their thoughts play out as actions. From then on it can only be refined, not re-invented. It is difficult to analyse this transition because it is instinctive, the product of the chemistry between an actor and the refining eye that focuses their performance.

Once through this week we returned again to practicalities, and Gill taught me the most important lesson I feel I have learned about rehearsal by running the scene changes much more than he ran the play, arguing that 'if they get the transitions right, and they're confident in them, everything else will flow from that'. It played out just so – practising the hard parts allowed the actors to flow through into the dialogue without thinking. The other great lesson I learned during rehearsals was also about pragmatism and practicality, and related again to dealing with actors, as everything does in Gill's credo of directing. Gill told the company about a documentary he had seen following the rehearsals of a production of *Hamlet*, and a section of the documentary where the director and the actor playing Hamlet worked on the 'to be or not to be' speech. The actor performed the speech, and then he and the director sat down and undertook what Gill assured us was a brilliant and fascinating dissection of what Hamlet was saying, what it all meant, what action it performed in the play and so on. At the end of this they agreed they understood much better what was going on, and how to do it. 'And then at the end he did the speech again and it was exactly the same as how he'd done it quarter of an hour before', Gill concluded gleefully.

The lesson, which I failed to learn when I insisted two years later on telling my actors all about Jeremy Bentham and the subjugation of prisoners by suggestion alone, was that an exhaustive exploration of the meaning and subtext of a play was not necessarily helpful to the process of putting that play on the stage. Only what affected a performance was necessary in a rehearsal room. When I began writing this book, I met the actor Kenneth Cranham, a veteran of many Gill productions, in a churchyard near my flat, and waylaid him. Speaking of the first production of *Kick For Touch*, he recalled an experience similar to the one I had with *Small Change* – he would search to discover the logic of his part, trying to understand why the play, mostly made up of short lines of dialogue, would occasionally break out into longer speeches, an experience something like coming into clearings in a wood. Gill stayed out of this. 'If he thinks you're doing it right he'll leave you alone a lot of the time', Cranham said. Because he had done *Kick for Touch* right, Gill had never gone through why he thought Cranham's character was saying what he was saying. It was already being done, and to explore why it was going right would have been irrelevant conversation. All that is needed in rehearsal is whatever is needed to make the play work on stage.

I saw similar games being played with actors while rehearsing *The Aliens*. Gill had an extraordinary sensitivity to the needs of actors – one of our company worked best by being left alone while he developed his performance, given room to grow through trial, error, and the accrual of detail, rather than a constant testing of his decisions as he went along; another brought an immediate reading that was enriched by the steady application of pressure by the director, a gradual layering of intensity achieved through repetition of scenes and passages in rehearsal; and the third worked best when responding instantly to notes, and so was directed completely differently to the other two, questioned and refined as he went along, transforming his reading as he worked line by line through his part. Gill effectively went through three different rehearsal processes with the three actors, discovering their needs and responding to them as he went, conducting a live and reactive engagement with the minds and bodies at work in the room.

The trick of this process, as opposed to a rehearsal process that prioritises specific rehearsal techniques and feeds the company and the play through them, comes in cohering these different rehearsals conducted with each actor into a production that sings in a single key. This is possible because of the organising eye of the director. The decisions of rehearsal are all passed through a single brain, and so maintain a coherent aesthetic if that mind is strong and clear enough to apply one, to leave a distinctive impression. Terry Gilliam describes film making in the same terms – in his reading of that craft, there is very little work to actually do. As a director, he just sits and answers a thousand questions, and because his own character has certain qualities, the way he answers these innumerable simple 'yes' or 'no' questions adds up to a film with a certain identifiable style. On *The Aliens*, this coherence was also brought about through the atmosphere Gill created in the first week of rehearsals, the shared frame of reference generated by poetry and time spent together talking in a room before the detail and the blocking began, on which the actors were later able to draw.

I came away from rehearsing *The Aliens* with a new, technically focused approach to watching or directing theatre. A practical grounding in what Gill called 'our trade' – it seemed important and satisfying to me that by working with Gill I was going into a trade, not an art form – gave me a new way into Gill's own plays. Those plays challenged, confounded and entranced me as complex works of art – but now I could also tackle them while bearing in mind the far more practical maxim Gill had offered towards the end of rehearsals over lunch one day that 'all you need to do a play is a couple of chairs, preferably slightly different ones so they look interesting, so that the bodies can make different shapes on stage.' This aesthetic was enacted in *The Aliens*, where our set effectively consisted of a couple of chairs and a beer crate with the audience huddled round on every side. Once the play was in production, the effect of staring at these everyday objects for ninety minutes under theatre lights was extraordinary. They became luminous and beautiful when stripped of their everyday context and placed on a stage, as my attention focused into a smaller circle.

This pragmatism has been one of Gill's great lessons for the directors who have assisted him and worked with him. I encountered the same practical philosophy in conversation with John Burgess when he advised me a short time after working on *The Aliens*, 'try not to write four handers, because it's difficult for the director to stop the actors from standing in squares; and if you do, don't write four-handers with no chairs on stage because then it's really hard', and again from Josie Rourke, who directed a production of *Kick For Touch* in a festival of Gill's plays at Sheffield in 2002. Rourke and her actors had been much provoked by a particular line in the play – the mother's demand to her son that he 'look at my hands'. As Rourke told the story to me, she gave great weight to this line in her reading of the play, and after the performance Gill's only criticism came back that the line hadn't wanted the significance with which the actor had eventually delivered it – 'it's just her telling him to look at her hands.' These attitudes, from Gill and from directors whose work he has influenced, where the artistry of the theatre was rooted in a specific and accessible detail were invigorating to me as I sought to learn my trade.

★

I should reassure you now that this book is not about me, and that I will disappear from its story as soon as I can. However, before I depart and allow the lead character his entrance, I would like to make one more detour. From time to time in the course of this book, in order to best express the ideas I am angling for, I have found it helpful to engage briefly with the work of other writers. And so I am going to send you briefly by train to Crewe.

On the opening night of *The Aliens*, Gill gave me a copy of Bill Gaskill's book on directing, *Words Into Action*, and I gave Gill a copy of the poems of Bernard O'Donoghue. It seemed to me they offered certain synchronicities with Gill's own work. A few years later, I published an essay about O'Donoghue's work in an Irish magazine called *The SHOp*. By way of introduction to something I hope to say about Gill's work in the course of this book, I reprint it here.

Bernard O'Donoghue's collection *Gunpowder* begins with a brilliant poetic establishing shot:

'In the cafe at Crewe, you can still feel
The old excitement of trains: a stranger's
Eye-contact, held guiltily too long.'

Perhaps you have never been to Crewe, but here is something that will catch you: perhaps not even the romance of travel, but undoubtedly the third line will chime. O'Donoghue opens with a universal – the rush of adrenaline he replicates with the caesura plunging us into 'Eye-contact' that comes from eye contact. We all know this feeling.

We are enlisted immediately in this poem. The 'stranger' is never picked out as a face or name, and so, for want of a signified, it's hard not to feel as if you have been cast in this play: as if you are the eye lingering over the lines. It is about now you realise that the 'you' in the first line wasn't a colloquialism, a synonym for 'one' – at the outset, you became a character in the drama. It is a subtle recruitment, but by the time you read the words 'too long' you are part of this poem – you have lived its experiences, and you are living them again now as you eavesdrop on a private world.

What is this world you have tumbled into? The poem suggests, not yet revealing. You find out what it's not as 'gradually the glamorous melt away/ For Lime Street, Euston or Piccadilly'. Decks are being cleared in the suspense of this present tense. Before long you get on a train, and it becomes clear you're an academic on your way to Bangor.

You start your journey, and quickly you're reminded that you are not really the subject of this poem – you are the strange, observing eye. The subject, a man in an Everton scarf who reads poetry in Welsh, gets on the same train as you. You watch him, and O'Donoghue has you assume that he is an academic too. 'But no: at Colwyn Bay, above the caravans/ And idle fairground stuff, he folds the book/ Back inside his scarf and goes.'

And suddenly a rug you didn't know you were stand-ing on has been pulled from under you. In the first poem of this collection you have been reminded that the world is larger and more various than your assumptions and understandings of it: that it resists your interpretation, and that this is a glorious thing. O'Donoghue has the view out the window put on a show to reinforce this point:

And at that moment – 4.30 pm,
On Friday January the thirteenth –
The blessed weather that had effaced
The long and horizontal English Midlands
Gives way to reaching bird-filled shores
Where winged plover vies with lapwing
To catch your eye against the latening sun.

As the Evertonian proves you wrong the sea explodes into your vision, and you become aware of the teeming and magnificent life in the world around you, that hides behind the details of the everyday, of books and scarves and guesswork, only revealing itself from time to time.

O'Donoghue has already told us by the time we read this poem what his book will be about. It is titled *Gunpowder*, and takes as its epigraph the following quota-tion from Andre Maurois: 'We owe to the Middle Ages the two worst inventions of humanity – gunpowder and romantic love'. This book, O'Donoghue suggests with his title, is an exploration of the solid world. But in 'The Rainmaker' we are shown that getting stuck into all this concrete is only really a way of examining the second half of Maurois' quotation – of reaching the abstract. The detail of O'Donoghue's scene is the way he chooses to get to its meaning.

By fixing his eyes on a specific, O'Donoghue sidles up to an address of the larger world that hides under the surface of everything. One of his characters finds a way to talk about love by talking about football in 'The Wisdom of Saving': 'I later learned that his letters from East

London/ About West Ham and the Irish rugby team –/ *And the Welshman is no slouch* – were covers/ For his love-letters to her.' The relation of these two letters is explored in 'Passive Smoking':

His gaze travelled up Murt's field
To the mountains beyond.
What he saw nearer I don't know:
A pheasant sometimes in November;
Occasionally a cold fox; a neighbour
Spraying a grey liquid across the hedge?
But always the same inexorable
Brown-green, rain-infested mound.

O'Donoghue's poetry concerns itself with expunging that 'I don't know' and replacing it with detail: but this always happens in the context, on the foothills of something larger. In 'Nel Mezzo Del Carmen', O'Donoghue engages with mortality through treatment of specific details: 'No more overcoats; maybe another suit, / A comb or two, and that's my lot'. These lines give us a measurable reading of the passing of life, a tangible way of engaging with an idea. In 'Pied Piper', from *Here Nor There*, detail is used again as a way of accessing a larger emotion: 'underneath his bed for twenty years/ He stored the timber crates that held a 'Simplex'/ Milking machine for the stall he never built'. The same thing happens in 'The Definition of Love': 'love most holds sway.../ In spending the whole time over dinner/ Apparently absorbed in conversation, / While really trying to make your hand take courage/ To cross the invisible sword on the table-cloth/ And touch a finger balanced on the linen'. Cohering an idea around the solid point of one finger touching another renders an abstract visible, tangible, familiar and affecting.

It is among specifics that our lives are lived, and too easily the details of our days can distract us from what is actually happening in them. In 'Orphic', O'Donoghue writes: 'I could have made an impact.../But something always came/ To distract me and take me aside'. In 'The Mark of Cain' he adds that 'people,/ Without any written instruction,/ Will look away'. However, O'Donoghue's work suggests that these 'somethings' causing us to 'look away' need not be distractions. As he observes in 'Pilgrims', 'We're never only driving to the sea, / But also on the watch for dippers, / Red-berried holly, bagged turf/ Or logs to burn, though we rarely/ Find what we are looking for'. The sea, that longed-for place you glimpsed earlier in 'The Rainmaker', works as deft shorthand for the motivating force in a life, the 'inexorable' presence in whose shadow we live – but it's the 'dippers' and 'cold foxes' that take up our days, and O'Donoghue seeks to reconcile one with the other, to turn seemingly small events into beads on a larger rosary.

In *Farmers Cross* O'Donoghue calls these details 'essentials which you can't go on without'. They are important, far more than simple ciphers for feelings. The poem 'Coronach' begins with the lines: 'No two told the story the same way,/ Even afterwards'. Part of what O'Donoghue's work argues is that if each view of the world is unique then we must seek to record them all in order to form an accurate picture of it. O'Donoghue reminds us that no voice is inherently worth more than any other – 'The shopkeepers live lives of their own'. These lives are important, they are the whole world to the people living them – a discovery O'Donoghue himself makes in 'Nel Mezzo Del Carmen': 'This road I had taken for a good byway / Is the main thoroughfare'. It is therefore as important to record the lives of shopkeepers as the lives of the great or good if we are to gain any meaningful understanding of the world.

It is very easy to forget the value of what is around us all the time. O'Donoghue seeks to give attention to things that might otherwise be disregarded: 'Happy the man who, dying, can/ Place his hand on his heart and say:/ 'At least I didn't neglect to tell/ The thrush how beautifully she sings'. In 'Rubbish Theory', he notes that 'things must first pass through/ A season of neglect during which

they're thrown out/ as rubbish, in order to become scarce
enough/ to be worth collecting'. His work, as well as
singing the praises of the everyday, also ensures there will
be some of it left for us to cherish when what
O'Donoghue has known as the everyday world has
become scarce and precious again. Part of the pathos of
the poetry is the scant likelihood of the success of this
venture – when he writes in 'Remnants' that he understands 'why I'd rather pay/ For these dying objects than
replacements. / I hoped thereby to bring back to life the
people', there is a sadness in the sentiment, because the
people will not come back, even if the world does decide
a few years down the line that they were important. But
the making of the effort is the heart of the poetry: 'Time
can be made to last: put on our guard, / We can number
every stone along the way'.

I reprint this here because practical stagecraft is only the beginning of what is worth knowing about Peter Gill: far more valuable
to me than the technique of his writing is the project it under-
takes. Like the poetry of O'Donoghue, it attempts to number the
stones.

2. DREAMS OF LEAVING
The Sleepers Den, Over Gardens Out

This book is not intended first and foremost as the study of a writer and his work. Before it is a work of biography or of theatrical or literary criticism, *To Bodies Gone* is a study of a way of seeing, an approach to the world I have found best exemplified in the theatre of Peter Gill, which is why I have taken his work as material. This book is about the use of art as a response to life, as a mechanism for clarifying and paying attention to the life that is going on around us by isolating what we love through staging it or writing it down, in order to pay it the attention that is so difficult to give to anything amid the noise of the everyday; it is about how that allows us to confront and make sense of our lives, and it is about re-living as being central to the business of living. It is a book about the way things become clearer when we look at them through artifice and re-enactment, when we take control of time by squirreling life away into the hideaway of the imagination. It is in service of this study that I now turn to *The Sleepers Den* and *Over Gardens Out*.

Freud wrote that the human mind erects screen memories around strong emotional experiences from early childhood, a defensive mechanism developed to insulate a powerful memory and the conscious human mind from each other. It can be illuminating to read a fiction in this light: as a fabulated version of lived experience erected as a way of viewing and, for the writer, reviewing a life, without exposing private experience to the public eye, or exposing the writer too directly to what Freud implies is the potentially destabilising or upsetting light of personal experience. Certainly, Gill's early plays seem to represent such screens: concentrations of experience that draw on real life and profound emotional experience, that perform some form of exegesis by allowing that remembered emotion to be viewed through the filter of a story.

Gill's first two plays reveal the extraordinary, 'bloody Dickensian' world of post-war Cardiff, a landscape reminiscent of Sean O'Casey's Dublin, filled with ramshackle homes, rent men and back-to-back grates, and populated by the lonely, isolated and frustrated working class: particularly by women, who run their families while the men go to work. This, at least, is the emphasis Gill lends to gender relationships in this society – women are seen in his plays to bear the weight of the whole family's troubles, while men are absent, silent, difficult to reach.

These portraits of life trapped uncomfortably in streets where it cannot express or realise itself also recall J.M. Synge. At the outset of *Riders to the Sea*, Nora says: 'there's a great roaring in the west', and Maurya speaks of 'the big world', an alien place outside their limited, rural existences where things are done differently. Synge's play documents the intrusion of that 'great roar', that 'big world', into the lives of his characters, in the form of a death at sea and the return of a body to a cottage. But Gill has a story about Synge's right to tell that sort of tale. Speaking of a meeting with the Irish novelist John McGahern, he recalls McGahern criticising Synge for writing 'as if he had a glass up to the walls' of the working class – as if he eavesdropped or looked in on them, without writing truly from their own experiences, in their own voices. It is perhaps significant that Gill might have remembered this opinion, because his own early plays seem like a striking advance on Synge's theatre. Here, we see the same social class depicted onstage, the same people rendered moving by the poverty of opportunity that has limited them, their lives remorselessly fixed by the conditions into which they have been born. As in Synge, they seem to live, or think they live, at removes from the world – it is easy to see the characters in these plays as set against the 'big world' that would have watched them at their first performances at the Royal Court Theatre.

However, in Gill's work, unlike in Synge's, there is no 'great roar', no author's narrative impulse superimposed on the lives depicted, except the impulse that stems from the isolation and frustration of the characters themselves. It is not a young man who is lost to the family in *The Sleepers Den*, but an old woman: the natural order of things is not dramatically overturned by the requirements of a narrative, but allowed to play out before our eyes just as it happens all over the world, every day. These plays offer a treatment of the isolated working class, silenced by their situation, which does not use them as narrative material, but attempts to present them as they are to be found living in any town in Britain. Unlike Synge, Gill writes of his own class, the world he comes from. The result is the presentation of lives blighted by boredom, emptiness and frustration, incapable of expressing themselves or escaping their situation, not rendered romantic by a narrative impulse, but told to us with an honesty of address that strikes me as profoundly and fiercely loving.

Ena Lamont Stewart, in her play *Men Should Weep*, about tenement Glasgow, depicts a similar class in similar trouble. Her play is shot through with a desire for escape, for alternative lives to the ones being lived by the characters. In Gill's work, that desire is also present, and in both *The Sleepers Den* and *Over Gardens Out* proves overwhelming – dreams of leaving are in fact the subject of both plays – but it is never given the outlet of jazz music, girlfriends or fashion that Lamont Stewart makes available to her characters. Gill knows life is not so kind to most. The mass of men lead lives of quiet desperation, and these plays reveal that truth beautifully and uncompromisingly, confronting audiences with a sad reality while imbuing the characters depicted with a poignant dignity as they bear up under the weight of their lives.

*

The Sleepers Den in an earlier version was presented by the English Stage Society at the Royal Court Theatre on Sunday 28 February 1965, with the following cast:

Old Mrs Shannon – Kathleen Williams
Maria – Jean Woollard
Mrs Shannon – Eileen Atkins
Mr Blake – Anthony Hall

Frankie – Trevor Peacock
Mary Lynch – Sonia Graham

Directed by Desmond O'Donovan

The present version was first presented in the Theatre Upstairs at the Royal Court Theatre on 18 November 1969, with the following cast:

Old Mrs Shannon – Madeline Thomas
Maria – Kimberley Iles
Mrs Shannon – Eileen Atkins
Mr Blake – Anthony Douse
Frankie – John Rees
Mary Lynch – Margaret John

Directed by Peter Gill
Designed by Deirdre Clancy

★

The Sleepers Den received its first performance at the Royal Court on February 28th, 1965. Desmond O'Donovan directed a cast led by Eileen Atkins in the role of Mrs Shannon. To date, this is the only occasion that a play of Gill's has received its premiere under the direction of someone other than Gill himself. His translation of *The Seagull* for the RSC was directed by Adrian Noble, but every other original play of Gill's has been first presented in his own production. This first outing of *The Sleepers Den* had a single performance on the set of another production directed by William Gaskill, and the play was not seen again for several years, until Gill himself directed a longer run in the Theatre Upstairs at the same time as his second play, *Over Gardens Out*, received its first staging there.

The play shows us the breakdown of a woman living with her mother, brother and daughter in cramped conditions in a Cardiff terrace house. There is no mention of a husband in the play – the woman at its centre holds this family together by herself. Mrs Shannon – her name hinting at an Irish ancestry, which is the case with Gill himself – begins the play by trying to engage with her invalid mother (a broken woman who we learn later in the play is in fact only fifty-eight). She is visited by Mr Blake, the club man, who comes to the house to collect a debt. Mr Blake, standing in for Mrs Shannon's regular club man, Mr Cottrell, who is ill in hospital, announces that he is unable to give his clients the time afforded by his predecessor to pay their debts, being under greater pressure from his own employers, and the predicament of the play becomes immediately clear: the Shannon family are living on bread, butter and water, without a penny to their name, and there is no money with which to repay what they already owe to others. On the evening following Mr Blake's visit, a woman from the Legion of Mary also comes to the house, hoping to call on Old Mrs Shannon, who the Legion has heard is unwell. Old Mrs Shannon does not wake, and Mary Lynch, the visitor, instead persuades Mrs Shannon and her daughter Maria to say a decade of the rosary with her. After she leaves, the three generations of Shannon women get into bed together, and Frankie, Mrs Shannon's brother, finds them there when he gets home from work.

In the second act, Mr Blake visits again. He informs Mrs Shannon that a court notice has been served on her by his employers, and that he is unable to help her. Mrs Shannon, who has complained of her nerves to Mary Lynch in the first act, begins to break down before us onstage, oscillating wildly from a desperate need to talk to someone to a violent desire to be left alone. Mary Lynch returns, and finds herself alone with Frankie, who reveals to her that he has been saving overtime money without telling his sister. In a beautifully deft instance of dramatic irony, he tells Mary Lynch that he has exactly enough money in his pocket to pay off Mrs Shannon's club debt comfortably – but he hasn't told his sister about the money, and his sister hasn't told him about the debt. Frankie also reveals to Mary Lynch that they have been served notice on the house they are living in, as the street is due to be pulled down – it becomes clear to us as he imparts this information that what we are watching is a disappearing world, a place that is about to vanish forever.

Frankie: This is all coming down, you know.
Mary: Is it? When?
Frankie: Well, we've had quittance. But they'll never do it.

In the third act, we see Mrs Shannon collapse entirely. Old Mrs Shannon has died, and her body is discovered sitting upright in a chair. Mrs Shannon shuts herself into the front room with the body of her mother, despite the entreaties of her daughter and brother who come to the door in succession and ask to be let in. Mrs Shannon, unravelled and speaking incoherently, makes to stab her mother with a knife – but either decides against doing so, or is emotionally unable to, and drags her into the kitchen instead before ending the play by stripping the bed her mother has spent her last days lying in.

The Sleepers Den is a study in isolation – of the way people become walled into their lives, their houses, their debts, their love and their language. Frankie, the man of the house, says at the dinner table in the first act: 'I had this dream... I can't remember it really. Something. About these three women. Three women. And three pains.' The play strikes me as being an exploration of certain types of untreatable pain, before it is a story told for an audience. Its narrative elements are ways of playing out the conditions that the three women at the heart of the play – Mrs Shannon, her mother Old Mrs Shannon and her daughter Maria – are living and coping with. In terms of plot, it is, as the synopsis above demonstrates, relatively simple – perhaps the most straightforward story Gill has ever told, shaped into a relatively conventional dramatic form with its three scenes and one situation, and with time passing chronologically as the play develops (a hallmark of Gill's later style is the inventive use of time and splicing of narrative order to near-hallucinatory effect, but in *The Sleepers Den* these techniques are not yet at play). The circumstances of the family are not conventional – they are not good churchgoers, and we learn Mrs Shannon has never been married – but this does not mean their situation is uncommon. It is a classic social realist play, staging archetypes and typical situations, daring the audience to judge them, asking the audience to

care for them. It is a play about women, and a family tied
unhealthily closely together by geography, money, health and
circumstance. It is also a play about a family who are almost
unbearably distant from each other. (Almost unbearable, but not
quite – because the conditions of the lives depicted on stage
mean that they have no choice but to bear their situation – they
have no way of crossing the distance between them or of breaking the ties of finance and family that trap them together.)

The play begins with a daughter attempting to reach out to
her mother: 'What are you crying for? What? You are, mama. Just
because of that. You are, I can see you are... What do you need?
Do you want the toilet?' Mrs Shannon's questioning sounds like
nagging – but nagging is always more complicated than it
sounds. It is always an attempt to heal or overcome a rift or
wound between two people, the frustrated manifestation of love,
turbulent like a river broiling when dammed, and so what we
watch as Mrs Shannon speaks without reply at her mother is one
person wanting to be loved by another. Old Mrs Shannon, lying
in a bed that dominates the whole of the play's single set, its
action and its meaning, doesn't speak back at first – the generations speak over her, and she seems lost in the room,
overwhelmed by her daughter's questioning. The same impression emerges from her son's attempts to engage with her.

> [*Frankie goes to his mother*]. Alright? [*She is awake.*] OK
> today? What happened, anything? [*Sitting on the bed.*]
> What do you want? What, love? Aah. [*He goes away*].

Frankie is helpless before the problem of his mother. He holds
out no hope of her health ever improving again.

> Mary: Is your mother any better?
> Frankie: What? Oh, aye. Yes. She is. She is just the same.

This, it is clear, is the best he can imagine for her. He feels powerless in the face of decline: 'don't worry, she can't hear. There's
nothing we can do.' He can only watch as his mother sinks deeper
into the bed that the horizons of her life have shrunk down to.

However, it quickly becomes clear that Old Mrs Shannon's silence is not all of her own choosing. Mrs Shannon forces a pill on her, and forces her into bed, for her own wellbeing more than her mother's:

> Mrs Shannon: Mama, I'm tired. You get in and then I can make some tea.
> Old Mrs Shannon: I've no need to be in bed.
> Mrs Shannon: I know, but I'm tired.

Old Mrs Shannon's silence in the face of her daughter's questioning takes on a different inflection. Mrs Shannon asks, 'Why do you talk under your breath as if you was afraid for me to hear?', and the idea crosses the stage that the mother is afraid of her daughter, though she might never have said so out loud. She has to share the air she breathes with a woman who, moment by moment, alternates from demanding that she speak to drugging her into silence, snapping waspishly, 'just you keep that shut.'

In her dealings with her daughter, Mrs Shannon's volatility and vulnerability are impressed on us again. In the second act, she teases Maria, telling her that she is not her mother:

> Mrs Shannon: Anyway, I'm not your mama, you know that.
> Maria: Mama.
> Mrs Shannon: It's true. I haven't been your mother all these years and I don't know what you're like.
> Maria: Mama.
> Mrs Shannon: Don't be so soft.
> Maria: [*Burying herself*] Liar.

The exchange is playful, a teasing that is the product of affection and that ends in an affectionate act as Maria buries herself in her mother's apron – but it is still, for all that, a compulsive distancing, a provocation of another vulnerable person through feigned rejection. It cannot be denied that there is an unthinking or perhaps oblivious cruelty in Mrs Shannon's treatment of her daughter, her insistent denial continuing until her daughter hides her face.

What disturbs this unhappy situation is the intrusion of the outside world, in the form of Mr Blake and Mary Lynch. This doesn't so much set off a plot as a pressure cooker. The people who visit the Shannons are as small and powerless as the Shannons themselves – Mr Blake apologises to Mrs Shannon when he explains he can't extend her credit or allow extra time for payment, 'I've got to take the rap for this street now and I haven't been with the firm long' – but they carry with them the tide of the world, which batters against the house. Their intrusions break the peace there, reminding the family of the smallness of their lives and provoking Mrs Shannon into violent moods. What becomes painfully apparent through the play's progress is how narrow Mrs Shannon's horizons are, how small her stage. Pleasures come in tiny forms – perhaps the saddest claim made in the play comes when Mrs Shannon says to her mother as she drinks a cup of tea, 'you don't know what you're missing,' before going on to decide 'I'd have another but I don't think I deserve two.' This is affecting above all because it is a common experience rendered remarkable onstage in the harsh, reflective light of a play, which demands that such a statement be contextualised, that its implications be heard, as a stage and the presence of a public audience always does. It is the language people use about small treats, tea or drink or cigarettes or biscuits, all over this country every day. When you think about it, it is very sad that people should live their lives so tied up in guilt and the rationing of pleasure. This is where Gill is at his most affecting – in his observation of the painful details of the everyday, his ability to point them out to us.

Problems and solutions, too, shrink from the existential to the everyday because of the scale and the setting of the lives in which they are experienced: Frankie, trying to make sense of a woman whose life is falling apart, tells her: 'you know what your trouble is, don't you Joan. You don't eat enough.' He has no thought of the real problem she is facing – no emotional or lexical vocabulary with which to confront it, engage with it, solve it. It is the sad and shabby scale of events that seems to propel Mrs Shannon towards her collapse: 'fine list of things I do, I must say. What does that add me up to? ... Look at what kind of washing up I do.' That her whole life might come down to the state of her washing up is affecting in part because we have seen the same concerns weigh down our own mothers. The play catches us up in a tidal wave of sympathetic feeling because without articulating its action in the mouths of its characters, it asks us, why are we living like this?

Being forced into a new awareness of the limited situation she is in, the extent to which she is trapped by money and washing up, releases powerful emotion in Mrs Shannon. Her behaviour towards her mother takes a darker turn: 'I'm not touching you now, am I? Bugger you, shut up. I'm not going to hurt you. You'll have them in from next door. I didn't hit you. I didn't hit you, you bugger. You bugger, I will hit you. Keep still, I will. You bugger, I will. I will. I'll kill you. God'll have you one day for this.' This aggression is matched only by a desperate need she also displays – the need for company, the need for love. Left alone, she becomes lonely, anxious, eventually almost hysterical in her need for other people: 'Maria. Our Maria. You're not in. Our Frankie. Frankie. Not in. Our Maria. Wake up now, Mama. Come on, mama. Wake up. Wake up. [*Desperate*]. Get up. Get up. Our Frankie!' Mrs Shannon even bangs on next door's wall to try and find someone to talk to. The same woman who shuts herself off from the world, who threatens her loved ones and seems to ward off all closeness, is suffering desperately from the lack of it.

The Shannons feel no sense of belonging to the world around them, and the intrusions of finance and faith remind them of how they are cut off, distant from the systems in which other people find solace:

> Mary: What do we know it as?
> Maria: Oh. We. 'The month of the Holy Rosary.'

Maria's wry, weary 'Oh. We' speaks volumes about the mood within the family – who never go to church, who hide from the club man, who can't quite speak to each other:

> Maria: Where've you been?
> Frankie: Out.
> Maria: Where?
> Frankie: Out.

These failures to connect are at the heart of their interactions:

> Frankie: Hey, our Joan.
> Mrs Shannon: Yes?
> Frankie: Everything alright?
> Mrs Shannon: What do you mean?
> Frankie: Today. OK?
> *Pause.*
> Mrs Shannon: Yea.
> Frankie: No trouble?
> *Pause.*
> Mrs Shannon: No.

They are adrift in their lives, bereft of social moorings. Mr Blake observes that 'the doors are always open on this street', but as anyone who has spent time living in enclosed or small communities will know, this is a misleading image. It does not mean for a moment that there is anything open about the lives being lived in the houses. Mrs Shannon emerges as a woman who has been walled into her life, and is suffering as a result. Her brother criticises her for the state of the house:

> Frankie: Look at it. What does it look like?
> Mrs Shannon: I looks at nothing else.

The impression given is of a woman desperately trapped, but not quite able to articulate how much she wants things to be other than they are. Instead, her unhappiness finds other ways to manifest itself:

> Mrs Shannon: I get very nervy.

Mary: That's awful, I believe.
Mrs Shannon: It isn't very pleasant.
Mary: I believe you have to fight it.

This small exchange has a terrible poignancy to it, as Mary Lynch speaks blithely about a condition that is crushing Mrs Shannon, unaware of the difficulty of fighting anything in the circumstances she is in. Mrs Shannon is defeated on a daily basis by the challenge of her life: 'don't ask me anything now. I'm not up to it really.' Instead of managing, Mrs Shannon resorts to sad denials and self-delusions: 'I'll give this place a good tidy tomorrow. It's a bit late to start anything now. I'll see if I can't change that bed and all. I did that. Then. Ours is a nice house, ours is.'

The play's denouement – the death of Old Mrs Shannon and the breakdown of Mrs Shannon – is foreshadowed by a gruesome story. Mr Black, after telling Mrs Shannon that she can have no more time to pay her debts, informs her that her previous club man, Mr Cottrell, has killed himself by putting a bag over his head. It appears he has chosen to do this rather than die slowly of cancer. The spectre of a man who simply could not bear his slow and sapping life any more is a startling intrusion, and Mrs Shannon's deterioration proceeds rapidly from this point. Her breakdown takes a fascinating form: in fits and starts, Mrs Shannon attempts to phrase a question, to put a name to the experience she is having. She tries to express her life, but the phrase won't come:

Mrs Shannon: At this time. At this moment, am I?

This abortive line, stopping before the verb, juts out of a monologue she delivers in Act Two as she rattles through the room. Later she encounters a similar problem; this time the noun won't come:

Mrs Shannon: I could leave. I could go. I could say. If I could get rid of this at the back of my head. That it doesn't matter.

What is it? What is the 'this' at the back of Mrs Shannon's head, and how can she find a way to deal with it, find the words to deal with it? She struggles within herself, so that the argument is increasingly lost to us, invisible to the outside world and consuming Mrs Shannon from within. She gives up on speech as she attempts to engage with her demons:

> Mrs Shannon: Do you? [*The reply is torn from her involuntarily*]. Yes! Yes!

Act Two of the play ends with her abandoning speech all together, leaving it because it is useless to her and struggling with her emotional condition, apparently unable to do anything about it:

> *She sits. She leans forward as if with a stomach ache. Rocks herself backwards and forwards. She hums two notes monotonously in rhythm. She stops. Sighs. She whistles a tune. Silence. She crawls into bed with her mother.*

This is an extraordinary dumb-show – an eloquent portrait of a woman trapped in her life and unable to escape it, because she is unable to express her problem, her life being limited by its conditions into ineloquence. It is these conditions we become aware of as we watch Mrs Shannon rocking, singing, lost to us inside herself. They are the same conditions that were impressed upon her by Mr Blake and Mary Lynch – the same conditions Mr Cottrell was unable to bear. Awareness of the world pressing in against her causes this breakdown, and it is this growing awareness and this oppressive world we watch, as well as the woman who suffers under their weight. Gill drives Mrs Shannon's fragility home with the final stage direction of this passage: 'She crawls into bed with her mother'. This is a brilliant, complex movement, at once elemental and instinctive while also speaking profoundly to Mrs Shannon's present conditions. She is unhappy: she looks for warmth, safety, regress, security, darkness. But what she is also doing is getting into a dirty bed to hide from the world behind the body of her mother, cramped into the claustrophobia of life with her mother.

It is in Old Mrs Shannon that Mrs Shannon eventually chooses to locate all her rage and frustration. The play concludes with a striking inversion of that climb into bed: Mrs Shannon takes a knife and goes to stab her dead mother, before deciding she cannot – and indeed, that she has been cheated of the murder by her mother's death, stopped even from expressing herself through violence. Before this happens, we have seen her turn more directly on Old Mrs Shannon, finally telling her mother once it is too late how angry she has made her, the hostility present from the outset of the play becoming active:

> Mrs Shannon: What about the time I was going on the boat and you made me fall in and I had to come home? Go on, get out. What about that pear you gave me and the caterpillar crawling out as I bit in.

There is something movingly petty and small about this assault. Faced with a whole life's frustration, Mrs Shannon has nothing but the small details of her limited life through which to express herself: so a vast emotion is concentrated into these moments, these slight memories that do not begin to address how thwarted and hopeless Mrs Shannon feels. The attack, which almost becomes an attack with a knife, is a familiar domestic recourse: faced with a life that has not gone how she planned it, the cause a fossilised social situation rather than the success or failure of any individual, Mrs Shannon is able to blame no one but her own mother for bringing her into the world. But such is the weight of the emotion behind her small accusations, she is unable to bring them against her mother until she has already gone out of the world herself.

An inability to express feelings and thoughts patterns the play. Throughout, we see the family and the visitors to the house engaging with each other through rituals, not through conversation, sharing without actually speaking one person to another. This is perhaps at its clearest when Mary Lynch persuades Mrs Shannon and Maria to say a decade of the rosary with her. Kneeling together, they say words that are not even directly given in Gill's script (the words are provided in a footnote), and the sense prevails that they are not speaking at all, nor are they closer for sharing something: they are locked into themselves, unable to actually reach each other as they all engage in a ritual they do not feel part of. A kinder version of the image repeats itself when Maria silently combs Old Mrs Shannon's hair. This is not a real connection between two people, whatever it looks like – it's something to do in the evening. But it is loving, and a need, a desire from one person for another is present on stage as it happens, the same desire Maria shows when she tries to wake her mother up or asks her mother:

> Maria: Are you bad, mama?
> Mrs Shannon: I'm alright. Go on.
> Maria: Can I see you're alright?

It is the same desire which Mrs Shannon rejects when she shuts herself in the kitchen. These wordless acts of communication and negotiation are how the women live their lives, trapped into this room and these relationships and chafing against them, unable to do anything about it, but loving and longing all the same.

This complex relationship coheres around the lasting image, at the end of Act One, of the three women in bed together. This is Gill's most eloquent stage picture in the play, his most verbose piece of wordless speech. Loneliness and love exist beside each other, obligation and need, as the women are seen to be trapped both by proximity and by affection. The play's close has Beckettian undertones, as Mrs Shannon seems to decide, like Mr Cottrell, that she can't go on, and resolves to kill her mother out of rage at her life only to realise she cannot, because her mother has already died. She must go on. So she drags her mother into the kitchen: she goes on. Or, as Gill himself puts it, channelling Beckett into the limited domesticity of the situation just as Mrs Shannon channels her emotions into small observations:

> Old Mrs Shannon: There's no room.
> Mrs Shannon: I know there's no room. Shift over and
>   make room.

★

Over Gardens Out was first performed in the Theatre Upstairs at the Royal Court Theatre on 5 August 1968 with the following cast:

Mrs B – Pamela Miles
Jeffry – Don Hawkins
Dennis – James Hazeldene
Mother – June Watson
Father – Anthony Douse
Shop Assistant – Roger Nott

★

The Sleepers Den would not receive a full production until 1968, when it appeared alongside Gill's second original play, *Over Gardens Out*, in the Royal Court Theatre Upstairs. Nicholas Wright tells the story of the plays' programming in his introduction to Gill's *Plays Two*:

> ... I was in deep trouble, having opened the Theatre Upstairs with three ill-chosen plays, all very badly done. I knew that my next request for a pay packet was likely to be embarrassing, and I had the sense to realise that my only hope was to get in someone cleverer than myself to help me out.
>
> Peter had just finished his third play, *Over Gardens Out*. I remember my intoxication at the grace and simplicity of the dialogue. Quite recently I came across my diary of that time and found that I'd written, on a page of its own, the phrase 'the beating heart'. I meant that the dialogue had a transparency that led me into his characters' inner lives.
>
> I programmed the play as quickly as I could, along with a revival of Peter's earlier play, *The Sleepers Den*. Everything went right for the shows and, after that, for the Theatre Upstairs as well...

In many respects *Over Gardens Out* inhabits the same
landscape as *The Sleepers Den,* just as the two plays would begin
life by inhabiting the same stage. Once again, the play takes as its
subject the lives of isolated people in Cardiff, and Gill makes deft
use of the conjunction of this small, enclosed world with the big
world around it. While the larger society the Shannons felt cut off
from was represented in *The Sleepers Den* by two visitors, in *Over
Gardens Out* this role is played by the intrusion of the news, a far
more regular and impersonal visitor to the two households
depicted in the play. The printed text begins with the following
note:

> When *Over Gardens Out* was performed in the Theatre
> Upstairs at the Royal Court Theatre two television sets
> were placed one each side of the playing area, against the
> theatre walls. They were each tuned to a different station
> and the volumes remote-controlled so that during the play
> the sound could be turned down except in scenes where
> a television set might be on. The sound was brought up at
> the end of some of the scenes to help cover the stage
> management moving the furniture, and both sets were
> turned up when the audience came in and when they left
> the theatre.

A striking frame for the action of the play, a deafening context
reminiscent of Willy's newspaper in Beckett's *Happy Days.*
Multimedia performances and the interplay of screens with live
action have become a regular feature in the theatre of the twenty-
first century, but this was 1968: the Censor had barely signed off,
and this kind of technical invention was not to enter the
mainstream for decades. This curio, besides introducing us to
what a radical, pioneering body of work Gill developed in his
time at the Royal Court, a subject I will return to in the next
chapter, is however of less interest to me than the role the two
television sets play in the drama: an innovation, after all, is never
interesting or effective for its own sake. It is useful if it helps to
tell the story.

These two televisions have a profound impact on the experi-

ence of the play, acting as a kind of bracket, an ironising element
that reminds us of how listless the activity on stage is in comparison to world events, but also reminding us how anaesthetised the
world on stage actually is, as mundane images and programmes
flash across the screens and we see the news and consumer
context in which these lives are being lived. To set off these two
elements against each other – the private and the public, the
apparently important and the apparently inconsequential – adds
a layer of meaning to the play which cannot be ignored during a
reading of the text. The televisions also act directly on the protagonists – we see what it is that isolates these families, how distant
they are, the wrong side of the glass window of the screen, from
what looks like the real world (and in *Over Gardens Out*, it is the
real world – competing because each television is tuned to a
different station, rendered unintelligible and confusing and
strange, but for all that broadcasting live television which, at the
time of each performance, would also have been being screened
into homes across the country. The demand Gill places on the
audience reads like a challenge: you think the news is interesting?
Watch the people who are watching the news. It is a triumphant
humanistic gesture, a reminder that real life exists and continues
in places where the television camera doesn't point, and that the
lives lived in front of the television have as much to say to us as
the lives represented on the screen. Jeffry says to Dennis at one
point in the play, 'the human body is a very tough machine... You
won't kill the human animal that easily.' This insistence is
mirrored in the act of staging these forgotten people in the teeth
of the television and the pictures society has chosen to value over
others.)

Over Gardens Out details the relationship of two young men,
Jeffry and Dennis, and their relationships with their parents. Like
the early plays of Stephen Poliakoff or Manfred Karge's *The
Conquest of the North Pole*, they document the restless energy of
disenfranchised, powerless youth, sketching a generation discon-
nected from the society around it, and desperately trying to fill
the gap the rest of the world has left.

This disconnection is not total – in the opening directions, it is suggested to us that escape from the enclosed world of the play is possible. Gill informs us at the play's outset that 'Jeffry is a Londoner' – but his parents are local to Cardiff, and so the impression is that Jeffry has spent time away and come back, while Dennis has not yet left home. This is the first time we see what will become a central relationship in Gill's plays: the friendship between a young man who has left the provinces to go to London, and another who has not. That friendship is repeated in *Small Change* and *The York Realist,* and in each of these instances the idea occurs that in these plays, Gill is exploring and imagining the consequences of a decision he himself took when he left Cardiff for London, looking at what he has lost, and what might have been had he chosen to live otherwise. The plays seem to act, to some extent, as a place where Gill is able to conduct a meeting he cannot have in real life – of two aspects of his personality, the man who feels connected to Cardiff and the man who feels compelled to leave. In Gill's own life that decision was made very early – but sometimes it seems in the plays as if the debate is ongoing. He has said himself that to go into the theatre is to exile oneself from one's own class, whatever it may be – and so perhaps it is natural that in his work he should be preoccupied with imagining what might be going on in the home he left behind.

Jeffry is shown at the opening of *Over Gardens Out* to be cheerful and companionable around his mother. He is a good boy, determined to iron his own shirt, helping his mother and proudly telling the baby in its cot: 'look at that for ironing, boy.' But he seems to know very little about the world he lives in. His ignorance regarding the baby in the house is comic but unnerving. At first Jeffry simply seems to be stupid:

> Jeffry: I think his nose is bleeding. Ay. You'd better come
>   here. His nose is bleeding. Ay.
> Mrs B: What! Jesus! Oh God! [*Goes to the baby.*] Jeffry,
>   you silly sod. I nearly died of fright. He's all right. It's
>   just his nose running. What did you say that for?

His stupidity leads to a more threatening action when, thinking the baby has died, he leans in and shakes it in its cot, and we wonder what Jeffry is capable of doing out of ignorance and lack of thought. The baby, like Old Mrs Shannon in *The Sleepers Den*, is a potent silent image at the centre of this family, negotiated around and cared for, but, for Mrs Shannon and Jeffry, not quite understood, and therefore not properly engaged with.

Dennis, on the other hand, is clearly unhappy at home, behaving like a child in order to spoil an evening for his parents as they prepare to go out. Dennis's mother tells him 'you always take the pleasure out of everything, you do. Somehow'. It is clear that these three people are living cramped too close together, that Dennis's presence is causing pain to everyone, and we feel deeply for the mother, as her son coaxes her out of her evening. Her husband, perhaps all too familiar with this turn of events, abandons her to deal with the situation as Dennis sulks, walking ahead alone to the end of the street to wait for her. Dennis makes it clear he does not feel he belongs to the world of his parents.

> Dennis: Where are you going?
> Father: I'm going to church.
> Dennis: Good for you.
> Father: That's where you'd be going if you had any sense.
> Dennis: Like you, you mean.

It seems, once again, that we are watching a family trapped together in a pressure-cooker. Dennis is a cause of distress for his mother, who tells him 'you've got me scalded... If I go to hell it'll be your doing.' There is weight to a threat like this when Gill writes it – his Catholic background makes hell a subject to grapple with, and not just invective. Dennis roams around the family home like the young girl Maria in *The Sleepers Den*, playing and trying unsuccessfully to engage with his mother. Like Maria, he tries to comb the hair of a family member, an expression of affection and love, a way to busy his hands and pass his time, but his attempt is less successful:

> *Dennis does her hair but gives up. He wanders about. He sits.*
> *Plays with his mother's handbag. Fiddles with the radio,*

changing the stations. He takes his mother's mirror out of her
bag. Puts her spectacles on. Puts her lipstick on.

The restlessness in Dennis leads him to provoke his mother
again, although this provocation, as with so many pictures in *The*
Sleepers Den, is a complex and nuanced image – it is also an
attempt to amuse his mother, to make her smile, and, most interestingly, to look like her – ostensibly in parody, but it is
undeniable that whenever someone dresses up as someone else,
an imitation is taking place that contains at least some degree of
sincerity, if the attempt is any good at all. In this dressing up, the
suggestion that Dennis feels distant from his mother and wants
to be closer to her enters the stage space, at the same time as we
watch a boy messing about and causing trouble. This attempt to
get closer to his mother, still masked as play, continues in the
aggressive exchanges between them.

> Dennis: Come on, wake up. Don't go to sleep. Mam!
> Mother: [*Smacking him.*] Don't be so spiteful, Dennis.
> Dennis: Mam. [*Tries to get on her lap*].
> Mother: Get off, you great lump. You're too heavy. Come
>   on then. [*She takes him on her lap, arms around him.*
>   *Quiet. He suddenly gets up and moves quickly across the*
>   *room.*] Can't you keep quiet for five minutes, Dennis?
> Dennis: I'm going out. Tara.
> Mother: Don't you be late, do you hear me?

Like Mrs Shannon, Dennis tries to wake his mother for
company – and while there is no bed for him to get into, his
joking attempt to sit on his mother's lap, to annoy and amuse her,
is in part a repetition of the image that dominated *The Sleepers*
Den – a movement towards physical connection as a substitute or
cipher for actual connection. On this occasion it doesn't work,
and Dennis, oscillating wildly from one mood to another, walks
out of the house, suddenly abandoning his mother. The gesture
is perhaps aggressive and hurtful, as much as it is thoughtless –
Dennis proves himself adept at these subtle manipulations of his
mother. Later, he resorts to the same needling tactic Mrs

Shannon had already tried in order to upset his mother, denying his relation to his mother at all: 'I believe you adopted me anyway.' But again, this idea, ostensibly a tactic, a military manoeuvre in a war of attrition between two people, is also seen to pray sincerely on Dennis's mind elsewhere, to be an evocation of a genuine distance he feels between himself and his mother. He also tells Jeffry that his mother isn't his real mother, and that his real mother died while he was young. This distance distresses Dennis, causing him to engage with and explore it in his attacks on his mother, because, as in the Shannon household, as well as being tied together by necessity, this family is also tied together by love. When Dennis's mother is taken ill at the Co-op shoe shop, his concern for her makes the love between them immediately apparent:

> Dennis: Are you alright? Ay? Are you feeling a bit better?
> Mother: A lot you seem to care.
> Dennis: Oh, don't start.
> Mother: You always used to be such a nice boy, Dennis.
> Dennis: Oh, leave me alone.

Dennis's attempt to reach out to his mother, interestingly, forces the same attitude from her that he has previously displayed – she compulsively reinforces the distance between them that he has tried to cross with his sincere question. She is as aware of it as he is, and powerless to do anything but reinforce it because she does not understand its cause. At the end of the play, we are reminded of the quiet, subterranean connection between these two people, which is expressed for a moment in the shoe shop. Dennis's father goes to make his ill wife a cup of tea:

> Father: How much milk does she like?
> Dennis: Just a bit.

Dennis knowing this while his father does not is important – clearly, he has done this for his mother before, has cared for her and tried to reach her, wordlessly, with small acts of kindness in the past, with tea, the same rationed love that was the currency with which Mrs Shannon rewarded herself. It should initially come as no surprise, of course, that a son knows how his mother likes her tea – people make tea for each other all the time. But when we consider that the husband doesn't know how his wife wants her tea, and turns to his son for this small human detail, the loving currency on which their lives run but which he is blind to, Dennis's expertise seems to have more meaning. The web that holds them together may look like aggression, but, like that of the Shannons, at its heart it is based on love. Echoes across plays such as this are a rewarding aspect of Gill's work – the impression is that, reading plays side by side, one is observing the same things happen in different houses across the same city, as a panorama of a world is allusively developed.

The play comes alive once Dennis's parents have departed, and we see Jeffry and Dennis together. These scenes are the heart of the play, as the boys spar and imagine and fret and chafe at their circumstances, desperately bored, trying to fill time or create adventure. Jeffry is the instigator in these scenes, as the quieter, more passive Dennis allows himself to be made into the canvas on which Jeffry's imagination paints:

> Jeffry: How if I wrapped barbed wire round my fists? Of course, I'd have to have a glove on and then – Or. If you put your thumbs there. [*He puts his thumbs into Dennis's eyes.*] Out they'd pop. [*He spars, playing*]. I could eat you between two bits of bread. You know. You could put people on the ground. I mean put their bare feet over a bamboo shoot and then in no time it shoots up and finds a foot in the way, but it can't stop so it grows through it... I should like to have someone in the corner of a room all bandages. They'd be in a mess after punishment. Or make you swallow a mouse. I'd like to tie someone up. Punish them. Belt fuck out of them and then tape it. Put it on tape. Then I'd tie them up and play it back. And then start over again.

This violent, indulgent scenario reveals a profound darkness in Jeffry as he seems to allude to the war in Vietnam with his gruesome bamboo story, and perhaps with his idea of taped beatings to the recordings of Ian Brady and Myra Hindley, whose conviction came two years before the play's production, is set alongside more mundane instances of youthful bad behaviour, as the boys steal a sheet from a line and then bury it, then steal women's clothing – and with less inspired attempts to deal with boredom:

> Jeffry: Let's go over the park.
> Dennis: It'll be closed.
> Jeffry: Not yet.
> Dennis: He'll be closing.
> Jeffry: We can get out.
> Dennis: How?
> Jeffry: Climb over.
> Dennis: You ever see me climb?
> Jeffry: Well, squeeze through them. You're skinny enough.
>   Let's go over the allotments then.

Jeffry also proceeds to bring some of his fantasies to life, escalating his threats towards Dennis:

> Jeffry: I'm going to keep a punishment book for you from
>   now on. Right? Naughty boys have to be kept in order.

And eventually turning them into violence:

> Jeffry: Now take your medicine. There's a good boy.
> Come on, hold still. [*Hits him.*] Don't it hurt. [*Hits again.*]
> Want more?

Still, Dennis remains silent, apparently no more than an extension of Jeffry's personality. Jeffry's restless desire to make something, anything, happen, set against Dennis's natural fear, quickly makes it clear why it is Jeffry and not Dennis who has left – although Jeffry's subsequent revelation that he is on amphetamines may have as much impact on these exchanges as the basic personality of the two characters.

Jeffry is at war with the same nullifying force that grinds down Mrs Shannon – the weight of his petty and tawdry circumstances, the lack of action, the lack of opportunities to escape. Where Mrs Shannon praised a cup of tea, Jeffry praises soft porn, saying of the magazine *Parade*, 'you don't know what you're missing'. What he imagines every time one of his flights of fancy takes him is a life brighter and more exciting, more dramatic and violent than his own: 'I was reading there's only two karate experts in the world. I wouldn't like to meet either of them. One of them defeated forty of the Japanese Imperial Guard single-handed.' These great deeds fascinate him, as does violence, the expression of himself that he can be seen to tend towards, once again perhaps as a result of his background, the conditions he has been born into – we learn that Jeffry, as a troublemaking boy, spent time on remand, and in light of that the behaviour we see on stage turns into part of a larger pattern stretching all the way back to childhood, all the way back to the heart of who he is.

Jeffry is drawn to scenes and moments where dramatic events take place, where there is activity, excitement or danger. In the course of the play, this leads him to haunt an old military site, imagining shooting down an enemy:

> Jeffry: This is where they used to fire. Ack. Ack. Ack. See
> the shooting range. Let's go and jump off it.

His desire for event leads him to not only want to be near this place where something once happened, but to jump off it – to cause a movement, an event, anything. This desire for movement is apparent in his interest in other people's sex lives, revealed as he regales Dennis with stories of his own:

> Jeffry: Of course I fuck my landlady... I love all the little
> birds in their curlers on a Sunday morning after
> having been shagged stiff on Saturday night.

The story may begin with his own life, but it focuses eventually on other people having sex, the more interesting lives Jeffry imagines surround him. This exaggeration of the lives of others also applies to Jeffry's idea of his father, who Jeffry dramatises and idealises gruesomely:

> Jeffry: The lavatory pan in our house was cracked. My
> father was straining at the leash when he had a stroke.
> The pan cracked right across. He died. There were big
> turds left in the base of it.

This might be just a story told to offend or upset Dennis, another way Jeffry finds of intimidating him, except that it leads Jeffry to conclude, 'He must have been a giant.' In light of that, the meaning of those turds in the cracked bowl change – they are another great deed, that Jeffry is drawn to think of for the same reason that he is drawn to visit a gun emplacement. Jeffry seems to be bitterly aware of the smallness of his own life set against the stories he tells:

> Jeffry: I read in that, it's against some religions to kill even
> insects. Even insects you couldn't see... In those places
> they think that if they take it that far somehow the
> misery most of the actual people lives in won't seem so
> bad.

He speaks here of another world, another religion – but there is a bitterness, an eloquence, and a pointed political sensibility in what he says that locates the emotion of the passage much closer to home.

The play's address is clear from this material, but what is perhaps surprising is that it is Dennis, not Jeffry, who eventually turns all this nebulous unhappiness into a statement. Having watched silently as Jeffry indulged in invention and bitterness, Dennis begins to speak in an extraordinary scene where all the play's characters appear on stage, in different rooms, speaking or acting simultaneously over each other. This welling up of life collects the disparate scenes and locations of the play into one profound statement about the energy that exists in the secret suburban world trapped between the televisions. It also shows how easily this energy can be drowned out and lost, how hard it is for it to be articulated – individual monologues interweave, with each other and with the images on the television screens, so that this welter of information becomes blurred and overwhelming as it is relayed, like a set being retuned and a programme losing itself in static. In amongst this sequence, Dennis finally speaks up, the centre of the play half hidden amid the noise:

> Dennis: This is me. Why did I do that? What legs am I walking on? Aching enjoyable. I ran. Oh dear. What was all that in aid of?

Dennis is commenting on a race he has just remembered running, but his questions take on a larger significance with 'whose legs am I walking on?', a typically succinctly and strikingly phrased evocation from Gill of a sense of dislocation and uncertainty in the world. This first expression of the question he has been circling throughout the play – because having the audience observe his intolerable home life is another way of phrasing that question – unlocks further speech from him, as he begins sparring back at Jeffry:

> Dennis: I should like to set fire to this city... I'd like it to be on a hot day when the place is at its feeble best. Look over there. Look at it. It is like a cave with burrows... I want to be in extreme situations. I want to be in the death cell or in the gas chamber. I'd like to kill you. I wish you'd kill me.
> Jeffry: I'll kill you.
> Dennis: Come on then, kill me.
> Jeffry: I'll kill you. You'd be scared silly if I really did teach you.

Once again, we see a person who is frustrated with their life, who wants something different, and, for want of anything larger to blame, is forced to blame the details of their life rather than their causes – in Dennis's case, the city he lives in. This emotion, an unhappiness in one's own life that is difficult to express or solve or change, is at the heart of both of Gill's first plays.

But what is it that the two boys in *Over Gardens Out* actually want? The play ends with a distressing suggestion, as Dennis's father reads the *Echo*, the local paper, to his son:

> Father: [*Reading the Echo.*] A cat. A ginger tom cat was found recently on an allotment at Morpeth Estate. Hanging by a piece of string from a bean pole. The damage is believed to have been done by vandals or boys.

Dennis stays quiet – what emotions flicker in his face are up to the actor playing the boy. But the play ends with a report, second hand, of a real action in the lives of these two boys, and that makes me think Dennis ends the play guiltily happy – because something has finally happened to him. What is more, it has happened in a different medium to Dennis's daily life – it has happened in the newspaper, the 'real world' of the media and the things that people read or watch. Part of Dennis's satisfaction, I believe, stems from breaking into this medium.

What Gill's play shows, though, as the play ends and the sound on the televisions is turned back up to accompany the audience filing out of the Theatre Upstairs and into the bar below or the night beyond, as Dennis and Jeffry are plunged back into darkness like extinguished Beckettian mannequins, put back in their boxes and bins, is that killing a cat in the paper is not an escape at all. Gill's observation is that these people exist, and that they are not escaping. They are being effaced by the uncaring world that blares around them, that is now leaving the auditorium, that is now buying a drink and discussing the merits of the play they have just seen. They are being effaced by us.

3. INFLUENCES

Gill's plays, like any others, have their various sources and antecedents, an understanding of which can inform a reading of the plays themselves, and I believe it is helpful at this stage to outline some of the context for his work in order to view his plays within the situating detail of their precursors and companions.

John Burgess writes that 'the three godparents who stand behind these plays are Anton Chekhov, D.H. Lawrence and Samuel Beckett'. These influences, in the cases of the former two, have extended into a practical engagement – some of Gill's most celebrated directorial work has come with productions of Lawrence and Chekhov, and he has adapted both writers for the stage. Perhaps surprisingly, he has never directed Beckett's work.

To say that a writer in the twentieth century is indebted to Chekhov is something of a truism. As a pioneer of the naturalistic theatre, Chekhov's plays form a central component of the context within which all modern theatre is made. Gill's more formally inventive plays can seem to be written at several removes from the naturalism of *Three Sisters* or *The Cherry Orchard* – although it would be relatively easy to argue that their formal developments bear some resemblance to the innovations of the naturalistic theatre, re-imagining the medium in order to make increasingly precise observations of the world – but Chekhov's great influence on Gill lies, not in stagecraft, but in a shared sensibility. Both writers are great documenters of boredom – of the limits that afflict lives and the way lives get away from you. They write sub-metropolitan worlds that gain poignancy from their relation to the great cities of their relative countries (London and Moscow), and detail the frustrations, dreams and ironies of people the world has forgotten about, insisting they are of as much value as anyone you might find at the ostensible 'centre' of the world, no matter how impoverished they might feel as a result of their distance from such 'centres', and their obsessions with that centrifugal idea of the world. Chekhov's characters tend to belong to a different class to Gill's, and in his 2012 production of *A Provincial Life*, his adaptation of the Chekhov story 'My Life', Gill made this point compellingly, flooding the stage with a silent working class in each scene change, who cleaned up after Chekhov's leading cast, re-arranging the world around them as they drank and worried their lives away. This, in fact, was an extension of a point being made by Chekhov in his original story, which was intended as a satire of Levin in Tolstoy's *Anna Karenina*. The inability of the central character in 'My Life' to feel at home and at one with himself in any strata of society sent up the same people Gill seemed to rebuke with the silent majority made visible in his scene changes – but it is a crucial difference that Chekhov chose to do this, not by showing us the life of the working people, but by ironising the middle class. It was among doctors, landowners, teachers and writers that Chekhov lived his life, and this is the world in which his dramas play out. Gill's background has determined a great deal of his creative palette, and throughout his career he has applied a Chekhovian sensibility – ironic, tragic, the largest feelings expressed through the smallest things – to a different social world.

In Lawrence, Gill found a closer precursor to his own creative project. Lawrence, Gill claims, was the first writer in Britain to stage the working class for no reason other than the fact that it was among them that his story took place. His characters were not a political point or part of a wider spectrum attempting to display the breadth of a society – they were simply his characters, and happened to work down mines instead of in offices. This was partly a product of background, again – Lawrence's plays are about the world he grew up in, so like Gill, he applies a loving Chekhovian eye to the world of his youth, making it beautiful and reflecting upon it through the distancing lens of art. He did so in theatrical forms much closer to those of Chekhov than Gill's, and so his great debt to the Russian is evident in a reading of Lawrence's plays – but Lawrence's transposition of the Chekhovian attitude to a working man's cottage was a radical and

original act, an extension of the efforts of George Bernard Shaw
to re-imagine the theatre and bring it to bear more directly on
society, making it socially relevant and bringing a new political
conscience and sensibility and a moral seriousness to the stage.
Alongside O'Casey, Lawrence pioneered the giving of attention
to working class subjects by the theatre. In his first play, *A Collier's
Friday Night*, he crystallised this project into a statement, when
one character told another, insecure about her intellectual creden-
tials and unwilling to speak in front of him, 'as much happens for
you as happens for anyone else'. Lawrence, clearly aware of the
political undertones of this seemingly innocuous piece of encouragement from a boy to a girl and the strength of the formulation
he has come up with, repeats it in the play. The idea stands as a
defiant, triumphant humanist statement, an insistence that the
lives lived outside books (or television sets) have value too.

It is sad to record that the response to Lawrence's play in his
lifetime later caused him to distance himself from the ideas in the
play,claiming that the date of composition was two years earlier
than it had in fact been, and that he had been very young and
'green' when he wrote it. The implication that *A Collier's Friday
Night* was juvenilia is profoundly unjust, but Lawrence's doubts
over his plays are perhaps unsurprising. He never saw one
produced in his lifetime. Lawrence wrote several plays but had
no luck with any of them, concluding that 'the audience is there,
what is lacking is the producer.' In a theatre still dominated by
diversion, the insistently light, and the upper middle class, his
work went unappreciated until the mid 1960s, when Gill made
his own reputation by presenting them at the Royal Court. They
were perfect Court plays, a ready-made literary tradition to fit
the Court's project into, contiguous with the world John Osborne
had given expression in *Look Back In Anger*. Lawrence had been
absolutely right – what had been lacking in his own time was the
producer, and it was many years after his death before Shaw's
mission to re-imagine the English stage led to a house progressive enough to recognise Lawrence's plays for what they were.

It was Gill who eventually picked them out and established
their place in theatrical history, and that should come as no

surprise. To a writer who had recently finished *The Sleepers Den*, directing *A Collier's Friday Night*, *The Widowing of Mrs Holroyd* and *The Daughter-in-Law* must have felt like second nature. These plays, intimate studies of relationships between ordinary people set in working class houses, circling the dreams, ambitions and insecurities of the characters, document a world similar to Gill's Cardiff. It took one to know one, and Gill demonstrated incontrovertibly with his productions that these were great plays.

What he draws from them in his own work is an insistent, defiant humanistic sensibility, which has led him to look at forgotten people and the margins of society in his work. As his writing has developed, it has moved away formally and, to an extent, in terms of subject matter from the starting point of *The Sleepers Den*, and the Lawrentian unities and obliquities of that piece; but Lawrence is still a profound source in work being written and presented by Gill today.

As Gill's work has developed, the writer he has most fascinatingly engaged with is Beckett. Gill's work represents a sustained development of ideas found in Beckett's writing – few writers have more fruitfully drawn on Beckett's later work to create new styles. Gill's first Beckettian statements came with *Over Gardens Out* and *Small Change*, plays which, like *Nacht und Trauma* or *Quad*, communicated as much through gesture and the repetition and variation of thematic or visual patterns as they did through speech. This musical process of deploying variation to develop a picture recurs in *In the Blue*, and in *Cardiff East*, where the interplay of different voices recalls the complex web of words woven in *Play*. While Gill has never placed his characters in dustbins or mounds of earth, there runs through his plays the Beckettian attempt to lift the lid off a life and examine the consciousness whirring and remembering beneath it. This is the unspoken gesture of *The Sleepers Den* or *Over Gardens Out*, but becomes more overtly Beckettian in the monologues laced through *Small Change*. In Gill's radio play, *Lovely Evening*, this process comes to the same conclusions as its Beckettian equivalent – pictures cohere into a single figure, and we discover that the undertone to the monologue has been the death of a mother. This is something else Gill shares with Beckett – his dramatic gestures can so often be traced back to the actions of a parent, the loss of a family member, something simple and tangible that we more often than not find we share with him, which is one way his work emotionally affects us. The same is true of Beckett – the wildest flights of fancy and imagination are often explained by the revelation that all the words were a way of talking (or not talking) about a mother or father. The connection is explored most candidly in *First Love*, which begins: 'I have come to associate, rightly or wrongly, the day of my marriage with the death of my mother'. The narrator explains that this is largely because of a coincidence of dates, but the larger association – tying the largest events of a life into the one association, the one body, the most familiar relation of anyone's life, recalls Mrs Shannon's decision, faced with all the despair in the world, to turn her knife on her mother.

Gill's engagement with Beckett is distinctive in a theatre that, perhaps as a result of commercial interests, has largely failed to develop on the ideas of that writer. Alongside the work, I would suggest, of Caryl Churchill, Gill's plays stand as an unusually brave achievement in this context – a body of work that has continued to evolve towards a more effective portrayal of the ideas contained in the work, rather than the continual restatement of an effective formula. Something I found attractive when I first read Gill was the discovery of a writer who seemed aware that the divisions, patterns and plots of the average play were arbitrary - because, allowing for the odd shift from a four act structure to a two act structure with multiple scenes, there is undoubtedly an 'average play', a framework most writers work within, on the one hand a formula which has been found to work effectively, on the other a cage within which artistic innovation is confined. Gill seemed to be seeking to work without reference to them, to develop the best way of making a statement. In this, he is a successor to Beckett, a genuinely formally inventive writer who has sought to advance the lessons found in the Irishman's work.

There are, of course, numerous other writers whose work is echoed in some way in Gill's theatre – by direct allusion, quotation or synthesis, or sometimes by being in sympathy with what

Gill creates. Some of these sympathetic connections can be traced in Gill's production history – in his forays into television, for example, there are interesting parallels. Here, in a medium that was not his natural creative home as the theatre was, Gill's selection of material may perhaps have played a little more carefully to his strengths and particular qualities. He directed Stephen Poliakoff's television play *Hitting Town*, the story of two bored and directionless teenagers terrorising Leicester, calling up radio stations to make claims about incest. This play, with its roaming youth and its scenes interspersed and organised by the intrusion of a disembodied radio voice on the action, bears more than a passing resemblance to the world in which *Over Gardens Out* takes place – that of the bored young, an area of study Poliakoff's early work frequently revisits. Gill also directed James Joyce's *Dubliners* story 'The Dead' for television, and this book, also, may claim affinities with Gill's outlook. As we have already seen, Gill's plays taken together develop a fragmented portrait of a larger society, gesturing at the state of a larger nation where the struggles documented in the plays are taking place while never withdrawing from observing the precise details of everyday life. This strikes me as a similar achievement to *Dubliners*, and it is a project Gill continued to pursue, like Joyce, through the deployment of increasingly radical formal innovations which developed from an initial naturalistic portrayal of a family in *The Sleepers Den*. The trajectory of Gill's artistic production does recall that of Joyce, though the results of his developing explorations are of course different.

John Donne is another writer who casts a shadow over these plays. That Gill should claim not to have been aware that *The Sleepers Den* and *Small Change* are named from Donne, as previously noted, is interesting – the former, in particular, though an accurate description of the room where the play takes place, is a striking and memorable phrase, after all. I am tempted to read Donne as an indicator of the influence of Catholicism on Gill, whose cultural background and subsequent equivocal relationship with the church may have led to a sympathetic reading of Donne's own ecumenical struggles. Donne wrote: 'I had my first breeding and conversation with men of suppressed and afflicted religion, accustomed to the despite of death and hungry of an imagined martyrdom.' It is easy to read Jeffry in *Over Gardens Out* as hungry for the same thing, and his author being drawn to the dramatic engagement with the problem of the human condition that was at the centre of Donne's work. Indeed, the central project of Gill's work – the attempt to phrase a question, to express a feeling and situation that will adequately allow the writer to engage with the endless complexity of the human condition – bears striking similarity to Donne's metaphysical struggle. Also attractive to Gill may have been Donne's fiercely direct engagement with love and the nature of love. Gill's work first entranced me for what I felt was its unusually direct address of love, and it is this aspect of Donne that takes my breath away – the intelligence tangible behind 'The Ecstasie', the extraordinarily clear voice singing in 'The Good-Morrow'.

Another relevant antecedent to Gill's work is the work of Marcel Proust. Proust is directly invoked in *Small Change*, when Gerard asks Vincent, 'did you look up at her window, her yellow window?', a reference to a sequence in *A la recherché du temps perdu*, and his influence runs more subtly throughout Gill's work – which is focused, like Proust's, on an exploration of memory, the reconstitution and loving of a vanished private world. In this, Gill also perhaps recalls another French writer, Alain-Fournier, whose only novel *Le Grande Meaulnes* details the hopeless search for a lost world of youth. Gill's Cardiff, though never idealised, is rendered beautiful by the knowledge that it has disappeared – while Gill's attempt to re-imagine it back into life gains great pathos from the simple and incontrovertible fact that it is impossible for him to do so. His animations only allow us to see into this vanished world with new tenderness, never to enter it.

Besides his own plays and alongside those of Lawrence and Chekhov, the writers Gill has most frequently directed are Shakespeare and John Osborne, and an address of their influence on his work is also of interest. Osborne's impact, as a contemporary at the Royal Court of the 1960s, is obvious and profound. It is often said that the 'angry young men' found their voice with

Osborne, but a reading of *Look Back In Anger* makes clear that the play is, like Gill's, as much a study of the voiceless and directionless as it is an attempt to make a statement. Jimmy Porter doesn't run for Parliament – there's no scene where he gets on a soap box at Hyde Park Corner. His arguing and speechifying fills the silence and the time in a run-down room, another way of dealing with boredom, of tackling the limits of a life. Gill's characters would grow more like Osborne's – in *Mean Tears* and *Certain Young Men*, where a different social milieu draws different qualities from Gill's writing. Acknowledging the influence of Osborne on Gill serves as an apt reminder that Gill's work is always a political statement. The act of staging a world and demanding people look at it, particularly a voiceless and neglected world that suffers as a result of the ignorance of the better-heeled people who tend to be the audience of the Royal Court or the National Theatre, is after all a political act.

Shakespeare, like Chekhov, is a practically unquantifiable influence on any writer's work: but as the scope of Gill's writing has expanded, the work demonstrates lessons that have been learned from Gill's long engagement with Shakespeare as a director. The first example of this comes with *Over Gardens Out* and *Small Change*, where the pace of juxtaposition between one scene and another, and the plasticity of tone and texture, as Gill moves from monologue to direct address to memory to action, and between different combinations of his characters, bears stronger resemblance to a Shakespeare play than to the plays of any other writer mentioned in this chapter. This building up of dramatic momentum through the interplay of scenes and voices would eventually lead to the vast canvas of *Cardiff East,* a play which, in portraying a whole world, certainly draws on the ambitious example of Shakespeare's documentations of the full sweep of society.

★

Gill's assimilations of the lessons of these writers have extended, in a few cases, to adapting or translating their work for production. Gill has enjoyed an impressive career as an adaptor and translator, an interpretive role that marries his skills as creator and interpreter and which has underlined stylistic sympathies between himself and other artists. This process began at the Royal Court, where he adapted Chekhov's short story 'My Life' into the play *A Provincial Life*, and also adapted Lawrence's *The Merry-go-Round* for the stage. *A Provincial Life*, which was given a full production by National Theatre Wales in 2012, was the first of a series of engagements with Chekhov's work – Gill would later translate *The Cherry Orchard* for his own celebrated Riverside Studios production, and *The Seagull* for a production directed by Adrian Noble for the RSC. To read these translations or adaptations is an interesting process of excavation, as one is able to see both the source of Gill's interest and the qualities which he brought to the work as a writer.

To my mind, the most interesting of these renderings is *A Provincial Life*, a significant enough development on Chekhov's story to warrant a change of title. Written in 1966 because Gill was, as he puts it, 'incredibly touched' by Chekhov's story, it was presented on the set of another Royal Court production for one night. The play came very early in Gill's career. At the time he wrote it, he was moving in precisely the opposite direction to the play's hero, Misail, who quits bourgeois society for the 'real life' of the country – Gill, who had moved from Cardiff to London, denies realising that opposition as he wrote, but the coincidence is interesting.

Patterned throughout *A Provincial Life* are moving examples of Gill's eye for the minutiae of human life – for care, worry, and love. People reach out to one another throughout Gill's work, and it is no different here – when Misail's father asks him, 'are you alright. You're looking pale. Have you been feeling unwell again?', a distance between two people is revealed, and their attempts to cross it, to care for one another, are shown to be snagged in the inadequate medium of speech. Misail says later in the play to his father, 'I love you. I am unutterably sorry that we are apart.' That 'unutterably' is at the centre of the play. Characters attempt to put words to the feeling time and again, however, because 'one must love. We ought to love oughtn't we?' This impulse, the need to love, is the motivating power behind Gill's work, and the materials of his theatre, the elements which complicate and humanise love, are the particularities of everyday life – Gill expresses the emotional trajectory of so much of his writing when he has Misail say, 'sometimes I think such marvellous things and dream such brilliant conclusions but my thoughts are always broken by visions of rissoles or bowls of porridge.' The movement from the idea to the specific that contains but also expresses the emotion recurs in play after play.

What we watch in *A Provincial Life* is a struggle to come to terms with life: an attempt to find meaning in it, to accommodate frustration and bear the fact that life is passing you by each second you are living it. Misail tries to drown his anxieties in work, but the attempt is a vain one. It is among the details of the world, the rissoles and bowls of porridge, that meaning is lost. This 'drowning' in life is inevitable. Like any emotion, a life is always caged into the specifics of a body, a home town, a world – but in Gill's work, the way that happens, and the way the emotion and life show through, become the focus of attention, making beautiful a struggle that might at first appear as empty of love as a pair of old boots.

This is perhaps the overriding reason Gill has been drawn to Chekhov throughout his career. The constant ebb of life, as it flows past and away from his characters, is distinctive in Gill's treatments and translations. Engaging with Chekhov allows Gill to come to express the idea that life and love are elsewhere, lost in simile, only recognised afterwards, seen across a distance. What meaning there is in Misail's life becomes all of these when he says, 'she is like a green parrot that had escaped and used to fly in the gardens of a square where I used to work.' Life and love seem very far away from Cleopatra when she asks, 'what is it that stops people from acting as they really desire?', not knowing that the person she is speaking to has fallen asleep. Gill asks this question in all his work – in *Small Change*, Gerard asks, 'what is it, what is it that will find the moment, that will...' That moment, that meaning, is elusive – but Gill reminds us that it is out there, hidden in the details of living.

4. THE LOOK OF DISTANCE
THE ROYAL COURT THEATRE AND *SMALL CHANGE*

All directors, during rehearsal, are engaged in the accumulation of detail. A rehearsal process is in part the accumulation of different contexts, frames of reference, banks of detail that the actors in a production are able to call upon and work within, honing and nuancing their performances as they develop ghost texts of actions, units and objectives to underscore the lines they speak; an off-stage life for their characters; a political and social context for the story they tell; a world of personal experience that is relevant or equivalent; a historical or cultural understanding of the world of the play and the texts that have been written about it or out of it. These frames of reference, complementary and overlapping, create a dense body of thought and gathered life from which an actor can draw and detail their work.

Gill's work as a director is distinguished by a minute attention to such detail; a numinous and imagist quality that is the product of the intricate rehearsal of movements and a visual aesthetic augmented by particular values in design and lighting; an insistence on finding the truth of a line, what Harley Granville Barker called 'the tune' of a line and a play; and, perhaps most importantly, a practicality that rejects all overtures to process in favour of an engagement with actors and text. He first developed and displayed these characteristics at the Royal Court Theatre, producing an extraordinary body of work in his early career that marked him out as a director of singular vision.

Gill's career has played out in four relatively distinct phases – a first period when he was an assistant and then associate director at the Royal Court; a second when he founded and was the first Artistic Director of the Riverside Studios in Hammersmith; a third when he was an associate director at the National Theatre, during which time he founded and ran the National Theatre Studio; and a fourth period when he has worked across Britain in a wide variety of theatres, without a 'home' theatre for his work. All of his work in the theatre has, however, served to develop and expand a recurrent and distinctive governing style, and is always a development of the ideas he first formulated at the Royal Court in the 1960s.

To address this work, however, we must first step back to a time before Gill's birth, to Croydon in 1909, where a twenty-four year old teacher is writing a play.

David Herbert Lawrence had been writing for five years in 1909, the year of his first professional publication (a group of poems in the *English Review*), when he first sat down to write drama. He had been going to the theatre while living in Croydon, and had been particularly impressed by Synge – '*Riders to the Sea* is about the genuinest bit of dramatic tragedy, English, since Shakespeare, I should say'. Before Lawrence, there was indeed little work that spoke as 'genuinely' as Synge: it was only after he inspired Lawrence into his own response that it became possible to see where Synge's sympathetic understanding of the working class fell short and became eavesdropping, as John McGahern would do years later in conversation with Peter Gill, and as Lawrence himself would later do in his correspondence – 'even Synge, whom I admire very much indeed, is a bit too rounded off and, as it were, put on the shelf to be looked at. I can't bear art you can walk around and admire'. In 1909, such qualifications were not yet formulated: provoked by Synge's example, and always possessed by polymath workaholism, Lawrence tried his hand at a 'genuine' dramatic voice of his own.

Like many young writers, he started by writing about himself. Unlike most other writers of the period, however, Lawrence's analysis of himself provided a window onto a world rarely visited in previous fiction: that of working class, industrial England, a world of miners' cottages and working rituals that, as Raymond Williams noted, Lawrence would eventually make the central subject of his work, but which he initially only approached through the writing of plays and some short stories, not through novels. The choice of a dramatic form to write in seemed to unlock new semi-autobiographical qualities in his work, and Lawrence wrote three plays in a few years – *A Collier's Friday Night*, *The Widowing of Mrs Holroyd* and *The Daughter-in-Law* – which, considered together, offered an extraordinary and unprecedented portrait of working class life in England at the beginning of the twentieth century. They mark a significant beginning in Lawrence's oeuvre: the start of his address of the mining country of his youth. Many years after his death, they would be recognised as the start of another, larger movement.

Not only were Lawrence's plays wonderful work in themselves, they were also unlike anything else being written. Shaw, in the nineteenth century, had written of trying to bring working class life onto the stage, and made attempts in work such as *Widower's Houses* to do so, and Synge had offered romanticised versions of Aran lives, but Lawrence was a new development: a writer who had lived the experiences he documented, not a member of the middle-class imagining working life into being. He spoke with the authority that comes from experience, and that makes itself known in detail.

He did not, however, speak very loudly: it proved near impossible to shepherd his work onto the stage in his lifetime, as has already been noted. In 1913 he would write to a friend: 'I believe that, just as an audience was found in Russia for Tchekhov, so an audience might be found in England for some of my stuff, if there where a man to whip 'em in. It's the producer that is lacking, not the audience.' For years, these words would remain the thoughts of another failed playwright comparing himself to Chekhov and blaming the theatre, not his work, for his lack of success: until, years later, a young man who had already written one play about his working class youth, and was in search of a play to direct, proved him right.

The trajectory of Gill's career begins with D.H. Lawrence, whose plays Gill introduced to the repertoire of the theatre, having been introduced to them himself by recommendation. Gill had been at the Royal Court working as an assistant for a little while when the BBC filmed and broadcast a production of

Lawrence's *The Widowing of Mrs Holroyd*. Gill himself did not see this, but a friend who did told him about it and, intrigued, Gill rang the British Library to find out more. Through the post, a book arrived containing the plays, which Gill read with astonishment. He took them to George Devine, who wrote to tell him that if Gill were to do them he would certainly come to see them, and not long afterwards Gill directed *A Collier's Friday Night*, his first directing work, for a single Sunday performance without decor on the Court's stage.

The full production of what came to be known as 'the Lawrence trilogy' followed three years after this successful outing. Between that first reading and the seminal 1968 Lawrence productions, Gill began to establish himself as a director through his work at the Court. His productions were overwhelmingly of new writing: plays by Orton, Pinter and Heathcote Williams as well as a Thomas Otway play and a reading of his own Chekhov adaptation *A Provincial Life* at the Court (also presenting his Pinter and Williams productions at the Traverse Theatre in Edinburgh), as well as directing Shaw and a play by Frank D. Gilroy elsewhere. It was the Lawrence plays, however, which made his reputation. The trilogy was heralded as announcing the discovery of Lawrence as a major British dramatist, and Gill as a young director of outstanding talent.

One of the cornerstones of Gill's subsequent visual style came about by recommendation during the rehearsal of these productions. Desmond O'Donovan, another Court director who had directed the first iteration of *The Sleepers Den* as a Sunday night performance in 1965, suggested at the outset of rehearsals that Gill might consider making all the business of the play visible in *A Collier's Friday Night*, by showing a segment of the kitchen through an upstage door rather than having the actors disappear to the wings every time they went offstage. Gill took up the idea, and developed it to its logical conclusion – the staging of otherwise offstage events in the play imposed real time on offstage business, and so everything else had to be subsumed into this 'real time', and the completely accurate business such a development required. Gill began directing the play so that, when the

father in *A Collier's Friday Night* took his boots off in the kitchen
in sight of the audience, he took as long as it took about it, while
the 'onstage' characters, those still in the room where Lawrence
had set the main action of his play, also had to play their scene at
the pace of this upstage action, timing it against real life. Rather
than decide an artificial point within this miner's house where,
because they were in the wings rather than the upstage room, the
actors no longer had to observe the rigours of naturalism, Gill
also directed them to perform other actions in the play while
offstage – so that throughout the run of the trilogy (it was not in
fact a formal trilogy, this was an innovation of Gill's, but subsequent publications by Raymond Williams among others have
treated the plays as such), a cake was baked in an offstage oven
every night. The action of the plays observed the unities of
reality, and from the small requirements made necessary by
making the kitchen visible onstage, a larger aesthetic philosophy
developed – a style concerned with minutiae, and reality.

In the age of weekly rep, of stock props deployed on stage to
give actors something to do with their hands while they
performed the lines they had learned that week, the idea of
baking a cake in the wings each night was painstaking indeed,
and Gill's work immediately stood out. Recalling responses to his
productions of Lawrence (many of which Gill himself had
reported to him – he became ill during technical rehearsals when
a stomach ulcer burst, and spent the beginning of the run in
hospital), Gill suggests that the overwhelming sense among the
audiences was one of recognition. People were moved because
they saw on stage actions from their own lives and the lives of
their families – lovingly rendered detail that seemed to have been
drawn from the lives of the mothers and grandmothers of the
theatregoers. Gill's work captured and, to an extent, because the
play was set in an earlier time than the years of its production,
recaptured the lives of ordinary people in art: given attention,
and thereby made beautiful.

What was moving about this recognition was the abstracting
emphasis the lives on stage were given by being presented in
front of a paying audience. Gill's productions never sought to

persuade their audiences to forget they were in a theatre – the lighting rig remained visible, and the audience were asked to watch rituals being enacted, not life on stage. He subverted his minute naturalism to achieve specific effects – when Bill Gaskill suggested moving a point in one scene in *A Collier's Friday Night* where a cup of tea was poured because the tea wouldn't have had time to brew, Gill refused, insisting the tea had to be poured on a particular line regardless of how well brewed it might be. The painterly, beautiful detailing of Gill's work came above all else. Gaskill remembers the plays, in part, as paintings, in which Gill drew out certain recurring motifs which bound the loose trilogy through a series of connected impressionistic pictures. The pale body of the miner removing his shirt and washing himself when he came home in *A Collier's Friday Night* and the dead body of the miner being washed by his wife in *The Widowing of Mrs Holroyd*, above all, seemed to give the evening coherence through the noticing and pointing of a visual trope repeated across the texts, a minute attention and cleansing of the bodies on stage which was also the governing action of the plays, whose progress detailed the lives of the people washing themselves and, in doing so, restored that sphere of experience to the popular imagination, the popular discourse: working class life was being presented cleaned and valuable on the Royal Court's stage even as the protagonists imitated that larger act by washing themselves. The first example given here, where the miner returns home and washes himself in the kitchen before eating, is perhaps the most celebrated directorial innovation of the productions I have heard of from the many stories told to me by people who saw the plays. Lawrence's text had a dialogue going on during the sequence, which appeared initially too short for the washing to adequately take place. Because Gill had made the kitchen where the miner washed himself visible on stage, this became a pressing concern – and so Gill simply instructed the actors to break the dialogue at the point where the miner needed to wash, to allow the washing to take place, and for the dialogue to then continue when the actor returned to the main space from the upstage kitchen. The amount of time this took is not completely clear – one audience member guessed in reality it might have been as little as a minute, while another claimed it had taken half an hour – but the specific timing is of course irrelevant. What mattered is that the miner took as long as it took to clean himself of the dirt of the day. What mattered was that the action tallied with the rhythms of actual life.

In the Lawrence plays, Gill had discovered the extraordinary emotional potency of life viewed through the distancing lens of art. His audiences were moved, not only because the characters were experiencing life in a manner reminiscent of how the audiences and their families had done, but also because these experiences were being taken seriously and recognised as things of beauty by being placed centre-stage under the bright lights of a theatre.

★

Following the success of these productions new opportunities arose for Gill, and he seized on them, developing in the space of a few years a rich and varied body of work. He began by introducing himself as a playwright to the Court audience, with his back-to-back productions of *The Sleepers Den* and *Over Gardens Out* in the Theatre Upstairs, before heading to America, where he directed a succession of Shakespeare productions and two plays by Pinter – a highly successful grand tour. He then returned to the Court to undertake a production which was perhaps more ambitious than anything he had previously attempted, certainly in terms of style – a production of *The Duchess of Malfi* which would introduce postmodern aesthetics to the English stage in ways not previously encountered elsewhere.

Nicholas Wright, in an essay published to introduce Gill's *Plays Two*, takes up the story once more:

> [Peter's] *Duchess of Malfi* in the main house was eagerly anticipated. There was a cast of sixteen, eight playing principals, eight playing everyone else. Bill Dudley designed it, with a line of salvaged doors up each side, and the predominant colour was ochre. In the Lawrences,

Peter had played with physical choreography in a realistic context: here there was no realism, instead a formal, almost mannerist, interplay of bodies, faces packed together like a Giotto. The actors were young and unfamiliar with the fruity acting that people expect in Webster. I can't describe how deeply the show was disliked by everyone except for a few fans. The critics hated it, so did the Royal Court grandees and the audience was mostly not present. All I can say is that I'm sure all the criticisms were very justified, but I'd never seen a show like that before and I've spent the last thirty years looking at bits of it repeated all over the place, in theatre, in opera and in dance. Peter had shot something new into the ether, and it landed. What it cost him was enormous.

The cost of Gill's bold but critically unloved *Duchess of Malfi* was paid emotionally, but also took a toll in terms of his career. He remains proud of the production, and the painterly style of his work on it – where Wright alludes to Giotto, Gill himself states that he began rehearsal with two images, that of a corridor of doors and a painting crowded with faces by El Greco. He believes – and Wright supports him – that he introduced striking postmodern innovations which were to have an influence on the work of numerous artists in future years. And he acknowledges that the production, along with the Lawrence plays, established the two polarities between which the work of his career would subsequently oscillate – the hallucinogenic realism of the Lawrences, and the painterly, Pina Bausch-inflected postmodernism of the Webster. But the production limited his opportunities at his home theatre – he would only direct four more productions as an Associate Director at the Royal Court. Immediately after *The Duchess of Malfi* Gill returned to Canada to direct *Macbeth*; in the following five years he also worked at Bochum, Zurich, the Public Theater in New York, the Royal Shakespeare Company and at Nottingham Playhouse, directing Lawrence, Shakespeare, and a play called *Fishing* by the American writer Michael Weller. At the Court he directed John Antrobus's *Crete and Sergeant Pepper*, Edward Bond's *The Fool*, and his own adaptation of Lawrence's *The Merry-Go-Round* before another project came into his life and gave him an opportunity to develop his career beyond the mild itinerance of the post-*Malfi* years: the artistic directorship of Riverside Studios in Hammersmith.

For a director who has been written of, at the height of his association with the Royal Court, as the fourth major influence on the Royal Court during the tenure of Anderson, Dexter and Richardson, this strikes me as an inglorious second half of Gill's career as a member of the Court's permanent staff, and a salutary reminder of the savage effect a critical bruising can have on a young director once he begins working on large stages. He would leave the Court to prove himself immediately afterwards as an inspired and inspiring artistic director, and I cannot help but wonder whether the same skills might not have eventually been tested and proven at the Court were it not for the response to *The Duchess of Malfi*. However, such speculation after the fact is fruitless, and would have been just as fruitless had Gill indulged in it when planning that production and attempted to play safer with his work with an eye to future advancement – the variables in the theatre are always too great for it to be possible to act on anything other than principle and instinct. It is to Gill's great credit that his focus has always been on the theatre he made, rather than the career he fashioned from his theatre-making. Gill claims he did not direct a play for commercial reasons until 2007 (and even that production, Patrick Hamilton's *Gaslight* at the Old Vic, gave no hint of being a commercial decision, directed as it was to critical acclaim with extraordinary subtlety and intelligence and featuring an unimprovable cast and design). His integrity as an artist has been a great inspiration to me and many others, and has led him to produce a body of work far more important than that of other directors who have kept an accountant's eye on their performance history. George Devine once said that 'the theatre is like a religion: you must choose your theatre very carefully, and if it does not exist you must invent it.' The theatre Gill chose to work in, which sought excellence above all, seems to me to be the most heroic, difficult and interesting of all possible paths through the trade: a theatre which needs to be constantly invented, because its aim is always to tell a true story.

Perhaps the best summation I have heard of the attitude Gill exemplified with the artistic courage and integrity of *The Duchess of Malfi* came from John Burgess. In 2012, Gill directed a reading of John Arden's great play *Sergeant Musgrave's Dance* at the Royal Court, a celebration of Arden's work in the year of his death. The play is Burgess's favourite, and was the piece he had chosen to direct when he was first offered a slot at the National Theatre some thirty years earlier. Gill, who was working with him at the Studio, was aghast upon hearing of Burgess's decision. Perhaps remembering *The Duchess of Malfi*, he urged Burgess to think about doing something tamer first time out and building up to *Sergeant Musgrave's Dance*, a vast and difficult play which, were it to go badly, might close the door on future opportunities for Burgess on the National's stages. Burgess's reply was that that was precisely why he wanted to do it: if there was any chance of him only getting one go at a National production, he was going to make sure it was *Sergeant Musgrave's Dance*. A refusal to compromise is a trait Burgess shares closely with Gill, and which would define their achievements at the National Theatre Studio.

Before Gill's departure from the Royal Court, however, he was to direct one more production, which opened in the Theatre Upstairs before moving to the Theatre Downstairs – a play that can be seen from the vantage point of the twenty-first century as the centrepiece of his career in the theatre, perhaps even his greatest achievement. The production lends the lie to any suggestion that Gill left the Royal Court devalued by the experience of *The Duchess of Malfi* – in fact, he left on a wave of acclaim and proceeded to turn a disused television studio, in the space of only a few years, into one of the leading arts centres in Europe. His valedictory production at the Royal Court, coming seven years after he had last premiered an original play of his own, was *Small Change*.

★

Small Change was first produced at the Royal Court Theatre, London, in July 1976.

Gerard – James Hazeldene
Mrs Harte – June Watson
Vincent – Philip Joseph
Mrs Driscoll – Marjorie Yates

Directed by Peter Gill

★

The seven years that passed between the presentation of *The Sleeper's Den* and *Over Gardens Out* and the arrival of Gill's next play constitute a strikingly long silence from a young playwright who might have been expected to increase his productivity after two well received productions in the Theatre Upstairs, which could have been the platform for a busy decade of work. Gill had other projects to occupy him, of course – his work as a director took him to America and Europe, into television, to the Royal Shakespeare Company and, repeatedly, onto the Royal Court stages. But I prefer John Burgess's explanation for Gill's silence as a writer during these years – Burgess has said that after *Over Gardens Out*, which concluded what he had to say about the world as a young man, Gill needed to gather new experience before he could make another statement. The idea, so clear in that analysis, of Gill's work as a response to and a concentration of his experience of life, is an attractive one – as is the image of Gill going through a decade of work at the Court, soaking up life, subconsciously collecting the material for what would be his great play.

The first striking thing about this new statement is the extent to which it is a re-statement of previous ideas. To a great extent, *Small Change* revisits the plot of *Over Gardens Out*, in addition to taking place among the same Cardiff working class and addressing many of the same ideas, hopes and frustrations. It even featured some of the same cast – June Watson and James Hazeldene played roles in *Small Change* that merit parallel study with the parts they played in *Over Gardens Out* – this was Gill's re-interpretation of a world he had shown us once before, a development of an existing idea, and a revisiting. Perhaps this is another explanation for Gill's long silence – if his subject matter was not going to change, then what needed to move in order to create new possibilities was the author's relation to his material. In 1976, opening in the Theatre Upstairs before becoming the first of Gill's plays to be presented Downstairs in a full produc-tion, Gill revealed this new perspective, as his play portrayed the world of his youth across a greater temporal reflective distance.

Small Change is a memory play, an excavation of lost worlds in which four characters each grapple with the problem of their lives, the moment that 'did for them', and the impossibility of ever breaking free of the limits of the world around them, of ever changing. Gerard, born and brought up in Cardiff, returns by train to visit his home and his mother, Mrs Harte, a woman haunted by the death of a boy named Jimmy Harrington and by memories of the past, who cannot forgive her son for leaving her. While in Cardiff he meets an old friend, Vincent Driscoll, who has been away at sea and has now returned to settle again in Cardiff. Vincent, in turn, is haunted by the memory of watching a young boy dancing to music, and by the death of his mother, Mrs Driscoll, whose nervous collapse and eventual suicide is documented in the first half of the play. Mrs Driscoll, trapped in a loveless marriage and unable to bear her life, is a frequent visitor to Mrs Harte's house, where she pours out her unhappi-ness and fear to a woman who, as Gerard puts it, is also 'slowly killing herself', letting life wear her down without actually falling apart in the way Mrs Driscoll does. As the play develops, we discover that Gerard may be visiting his mother because she is ill, dying even – the idea emerges that what we watch during the play are memories prompted by several train journeys home to Cardiff from London, as Gerard shuttles back and forth, and his mother slowly dies. It emerges, though, that there are other ties drawing him back to Cardiff – drinking with Vincent, Gerard remembers a time when they were lovers, is told it was him who 'did for' Vincent, claims to have been the dancing boy (though

Vincent says this was impossible) and turns on his friend for marrying, for having a life after he left Cardiff. The portrait allusively develops of a man who is tethered to the scene of his childhood, who cannot escape his past, and through its four voices the play asks a vast and moving question – what is it that made us like we are? That meant we lived these lives and not others? When was the moment we became these people, with these obsessions and these fates?

The play begins with a series of monologues from each of the characters. First, we have Gerard engaging with memory:

> Gerard: It was clean. I make that up. But it was. I'll make it up.

The Beckettian undertones of this, as Gill alludes to the closing lines of *The Unnameable*, 'I can't go on, I must go on, I'll go on', hint at the sense of compulsion behind Gerard's remembering throughout the play. Gerard fights to breathe life into memories drawn, not from within himself, but from photographs:

> Gerard: And there was a garden front and back. Two photographs show that. And I know there were roses... In one photograph, a woman standing in front of the house. In one of the photographs, a woman is standing behind an iron gate on the path in front of the house, with this bundle, this child, this young scowling woman's arms.

Here, he introduces the play's double subject. The real narrative focus is not the two young men, re-incarnated nine years after their more youthful iterations appeared in *Over Gardens Out* and struggling to reconcile a past which, in that play, they longed to throw off, but which they now feel both distant from and still as connected to as ever, envisaging the past as a lost, loved thing. The primary focus of the plot of *Small Change* is the 'young scowling woman' in the photograph – or rather, the two women, Mrs Harte and Mrs Driscoll, whose deaths Vincent and Gerard

are powerless to stop. The second narrative strand comes from
the fact that these lives are not simply enacted – they are remembered. It is the sons of these two women who do the
remembering, and so a second narrative layer, complicating and
distancing, is imposed over the first, and what we watch is both
the memory itself and also the act of remembering, presented
simultaneously on stage. As well as the memory of a story, then,
the recollections of the two men become an attempt to make
sense of the impenetrable 'bundle' of the self, tied up in the lives
of these mothers, sought for through memories of them.

Mrs Harte begins the play by remembering brighter days,
louder noises, times when activity and sound disrupted the
routine of her life. Just as Jeffry in *Over Gardens Out* is drawn to
gun emplacements, so Mrs Harte can't stop thinking about the
war:

> Mrs Harte: There was an air-strip over there during the
> war. I used to stand in the landing window waiting for
> the siren to go off, and look out... Do you remember
> the German plane that made a landing there? ...Then
> after that they built a big wind tunnel there. That was
> an awful noise too... What? Oh, he really was. He was
> lost at sea. The war finished me off. It started every-
> thing, and it ended everything.

What Mrs Harte remembers is noise and the anticipation of
noise – sensory experiences that lifted her out of the routine and
tedium of her life. She introduces us to the idea that dominates
the play – the search for the moment that defined the lives of
each character. Mrs Harte, the play's pragmatist, proves accurate
self-diagnoser when she decides it was the war that defined her–
and with it, the loss of a man, Jimmy Harrington, who she calls 'a
lovely boy', whose fascination for her is difficult to determine.
Was he the man she should have married, perhaps?

There are striking continuities between *Small Change* and
Gill's previous two plays. The play is, once again, a study of
people who feel trapped into insignificance. The two women in
the story live within the same constraints experienced by the

Shannons – Frankie's hidden money is recalled when Mrs Driscoll tells Mrs Harte about her husband coming home from the pub, and says that 'he hung his coat on a hook in the passage and nearly twenty pounds fell out of it.' Both fear the visit of the rent man – Mrs Driscoll also opens the play in a panic because she fears she may be pregnant, a condition that elicits immediate sympathy, concern and dismay from Mrs Harte. Another mouth to feed would have a profound impact on this impoverished world. Mrs Harte also has a method of dealing with the pressures of her days familiar from *The Sleepers Den*, revealed when Gerard chastises her for taking sleeping pills during the day.

Mrs Harte, like Mrs Shannon in *The Sleepers Den* or Dennis in *Over Gardens Out*, displays an inability to live either with or without her family:

> Mrs Harte: When they're gone, I get lonely. But as soon as
>   they're in again I think, Oh, Christ, why don't you all
>   go out and leave us alone?

The relationships of both mothers with their sons are defined by failures to connect and engage rather than real conversations. Mrs Driscoll struggles to get a straight answer out of Vincent, who stops talking when he doesn't want to speak to her, disengaging from the conversation and becoming another silent, uncooperative family member, a problem to be negotiated around like Old Mrs Shannon or the baby Jeffry doesn't know how to care for, or the bundle Gerard sees in the photograph at the beginning of the play:

> Mrs Driscoll: Have you been swimming?
> Vincent: Yeah.
> Mrs Driscoll: Have you been over the dock? Have you?
>   You wait till your father comes in.

Gerard, on the other hand, parades his opposition in front of his mother, divisive, playing a game like Dennis does:

> Mrs Harte: What did you say?

Gerard: You heard.
Mrs Harte: What did you say?
Gerard: You heard that, too.

The similarity does not end there. Later in the play, material from *Over Gardens Out* is re-written as Mrs Harte and Gerard go out into town (just as Dennis and his mother went to the Co-op shoe shop), only for Mrs Harte to get ill and need to sit down. This is perhaps the most striking repetition between the three plays. It is the first time Gill seems to toy with the idea of writing alternative lives, alternative treatments of the same lived experience, something he will later explore more fully with *In the Blue*. Elsewhere in the plays, similarities serve to suggest a shared world for the different characters, a larger story Gill is dipping into that gives context and colour to his dramas. This repetition suggests part of Gill's work is the revisiting of particular sequences and ideas, an obsessive re-engagement with past experience in an attempt to make sense of it, to love it, or to use it to make a statement.

The similarities continue in the relationship between Gerard and Vincent, who could be said to resemble an older, more defeated Jeffry and Dennis. One conversation between them seems almost to have been lifted from *Over Gardens Out*:

Vincent: Let's go down the park.
Gerard: The gate'll be shut.
Vincent: Let's go over the warmies.
Gerard: Aw. No.
Vincent: Let's go over the white-washed wall.
Gerard: What for?
Vincent: I don't know.
Gerard: Let's go over the park.
Vincent: Come on then. We'll climb over. Come on.
Gerard: No. The parkie'll see us.
Vincent: No he won't. We'll climb over.
Gerard: I can't.
Vincent: We'll squeeze through. You're skinny enough.

This sequence, a bored filling of time, is the same one that leads Jeffry and Dennis to steal a sheet off a washing line. Later in the play, Gerard is seen to be searching for significance in his life, just as the boys in *Over Gardens Out* sought an event worthy of the newspaper:

> Gerard: Now a star, X distance from the earth is, when seen by us, Y times in its past. Right?
>
> Vincent: So what?
>
> Gerard: Do you agree?
>
> Vincent: Aye.
>
> Gerard: So that the world being X distance from the star would therefore from the star's point of view be Y times in its past. Do you agree.
>
> Vincent: Nah. Well, in the idea.
>
> Gerard: So if we were up there, we could be seeing, well, we, we'd be seeing anything. Something in the past, any road.
>
> Vincent: What?
>
> Gerard: Something. Depends. Something. Pyramids. Anything. Something. A man's life must be in existence for all time, this must be.

Vincent refuses to engage with this flight of fancy as the two boys lie staring at the sky together, but Gerard is hard at work trying to convince himself that no matter what he actually does with it, his life still has significance. It exists, after all, and if he can believe that means it is part of the larger universe, that seems like some compensation for how little he has been able to do with it.

The new element in *Small Change* lies with the characters' greater ability to speak about the problems they are confronting. Where the inarticulacy of Gill's characters was at the heart of the earlier plays, here they work towards an expression of the problems limiting and defining them, attempting to confront and rationalise their situation. This is seen in the exchanges between Gerard and Mrs Harte. Where Mrs Shannon and Maria or Dennis and his mother have their most memorable exchanges through wordless sequences (Maria burying herself in her mother, Dennis sitting on his mother's lap), Gerard and Mrs Harte argue extensively, and bring up the problems concerning them:

> Mrs Harte: I couldn't get you out of my sight at one time,
>   now I think you've run away for good.
> Gerard: What say?
> Mrs Harte: You're drifting away from me.
> Gerard: I'm here, aren't I?
> Mrs Harte: But you're drifting away from me.

Mrs Harte's complaint is not exclusive to her – that drift, the growing distance between Gerard and his past, is at the centre of the play. She is able to challenge it, to try and give a shape and origin to it:

> Mrs Harte: When you ran away.
> Gerard: What?
> Mrs Harte: You ran away.
> Gerard: I didn't run away.

Her confrontational questioning forces further eloquence from Gerard, as he tries to answer what his mother asks. In doing so, he comes to the same conclusion Mrs Shannon came to when she made to stab her mother:

> Mrs Harte: What have you come back for?
> Gerard: Because you're the only thing I have to show off
>   with – you're the only thing that contents me. You're
>   the only thing I have. That's all I have. It's all I have.
>   You're all I have.

With this despairing summation of Gerard's life, we have come a long way from Maria brushing her grandmother's hair, or Dennis brushing his mother's hair and giving up. We see a young man attempting to get to grips with what makes him unhappy – a young man attempting to speak.

The play proceeds through a fragmentary sequence of interactions and half-interactions, as the characters succumb to the flood of memory. The effect of the play's exchanges as they build one upon the other is overwhelming, and described by Vincent and Gerard in the text as a blush of colour:

> Vincent: Everything went red as they tipped slag on to the foreshore. When they do that, suddenly, without a sound, the sky goes red... Across the backs, lights through the curtains made the windows different colours.

Gerard later invokes the same image:

> Gerard: When they tip slag on the foreshore, the whole place floods red.

The explosion of colour into the sky described here is one instance in the text where Gill seems to describe the flowering of memories and events on stage – another comes when Vincent kneels down in front of a fire:

> Vincent: I destroyed shapes that the burning coal was making, watched it forming a new mass, then destroyed that.

This comes very close to the pattern of memories that makes up the play – the presentation, repetition and variation of different shapes springing up under the light of Gerard's attention, animating his memory before being replaced by another sequence, another burning shape.

It is Gerard's remembering (and his revisiting Cardiff by train) that structures and drives the play, providing its overriding narrative direction. The struggle to locate identity is shared by every character in the play, but it is Gerard that leads us through it. The play is punctuated and driven by a series of extraordinary, poetic monologues, a new voice in Gill's work, first glimpsed in Dennis's speech about running in *Over Gardens Out* but now revealing itself in full:

> Gerard: Over the tide-field. Past dismantled allotments.
> Currant bushes gone to see with flowers growing in
> them from seed blown into them. Bits of the war...
> Pull up a tuft of coarse grass to see if there's a curlew
> nest. Nothing there. That's where they lay eggs. Lie by
> the river. Steep, gleaming mud. Wide empty river and
> then in no time a full tide, swelling, catching the sun.

The sequences begin descriptively, with direct observations of
Gerard's train journeys, but quickly develop into memory and
then into imagination – here, the idea of the war sends Gerard
burrowing back into the past, an active memory, a different day.
As the speeches progress, this regression begins to take on the
qualities of a search, as Gerard seems to be trying to locate a
particular memory:

> Gerard: Or earlier. Lost, crawling up the beach, under the
> legs of tethered horses. Shore, ribbed like the roof of
> a huge mouth. The grey sea filling abandoned holes.
> Ma ma ma Mam...

The plaintive cry that ends this sequence, as the eloquent
voice collapses into the sound of a boy calling for his mother,
seems to suggest the direction of this search. But it changes
direction, veering away from the pursuit of Gerard's mother.
Following a remembered exchange which ends with Mrs Harte
asking a younger Gerard, 'where have you been?', Gerard
grapples to answer a different question:

> Gerard: Perhaps I'd been over the park, or into town, or
> with Vincent, or out, or lying under the tree. Or down
> the field, lying under the tree, eating banana
> sandwiches or hanging about or deliberately wasting
> time, deliberately creating tedium. Or over the park,
> having squeezed through the railings rather than go
> through the gate, and having squeezed through the
> railings, climbed up and sat on the railway embank-
> ment, above the bushes and birch trees, and looked

down onto the soccer pitches and having walked
along the line above the playground, sat above the
other pitches and seen the whole plan of the park.

But the answer won't quite come – the passage ends with a
fading 'I forgot...', as another movement through memory comes
to nothing, to an unfinished statement, an unexpressed feeling.
This failure becomes the subject of the monologues as we
progress through the play:

Gerard: The afternoon was... It's evening anyway, almost
very near. The afternoon... It was evening, it was
evening. Got out of bed. This is intolerable. And
picked up a milk bottle. Stop... Where was I? You're
dying, talking, experience hoarded is death. Thou
shalt not take to thyself any graven thing nor the
likeness of anything which is in the Heavens above or
the earth beneath. Thou shalt not adore them not
serve them.

The idea emerges that it is not a particular thing Gerard is
trying to remember that is the focus of these sequences, but the
act of remembering itself, of re-immersion, that is Gerard's
focus. He seems to torture himself with this quoted command-
ment, as he holds up his own memories as idols, and the process
seems to strain him – a later sequence begins, 'I'm exhausted
looking out of train windows'. And yet still, he continues to
tunnel back into his past as his train tunnels through the air,
living the days again that he has left behind him.

What he is looking for, as Mrs Harte first tells us, is the
moment that 'did for him'. While Mrs Harte knows she can locate
the centre of her life in the years of the war, for Gerard this
subject is introduced askance, through the remembering of a
strange exchange on a train:

Gerard: He was sitting opposite me. He sat sprawled, legs
apart... I look like my mother in every way except for
her hair, he said. You've got it. He leant forward,

grabbing. Where did you get it, he said.

It is this attribution of possession from this drunk soldier, alongside the two photographs Gerard begins the play by interrogating, which sets off the process of the drama. It leads Gerard to ask:

> Gerard: Whose face did my grin start on? On what face
> will it end?... What is it, what is it that will, will find the
> moment, that will... What is it, what is it that will, will
> find the moment, that will...? Did a woman ever live
> who wasn't slowly killing herself, smoothing her
> backside lightly as if going to sit down and saying, I'm
> all bleeding?

Faced with this dense weight of insistent, presently unanswered questions, Gerard begins returning to his past, reliving old occasions and trying, as Mrs Harte seems to have been able to do, to locate himself.

Like Mrs Shannon in *The Sleepers Den*, Gerard can't quite articulate the problem that concerns him. Language fails him as his sentence – 'what is it, what is it that will, will find the moment, that will...' breaks down and has to be repeated, without any further progress. There is a new articulacy to Gerard though, viewed alongside Gill's previous characters, a seriousness of engagement with the problem of himself that takes him further than Mrs Shannon was able to go. Without quite expressing the link, Gerard, like Mrs Shannon, finds his thoughts deflected to the thought of his mother, the woman smoothing her backside whose invocation follows his failed question. In fractious, disjointed conversations with her, he tries to get to the heart of the inheritance he has from her:

> Gerard: I've become what? An imitation of what you're
> not actually yourself. You had better die. There's got to
> be a moment. Do you remember it? I saw you decide
> it was all up for you, I observed, eating the sides of
> that cream-and-green pram. Do you? Do you, eh?

> You had better die.
> Mrs Harte: I don't want to die! I want to take part.

In Gerard's mind, there was a moment when Mrs Harte was 'done for', and there is a connection between his own life and the aspirations and failures of a life that came before him.

While Gerard locates the source of his life, or perhaps it would be more accurate to say his love, with his mother, Vincent makes a different claim. Vincent's own memory of the moment that 'did for him' begins as narrative, a story told at the play's opening:

> Vincent: I switched the radio over and then I switched it off. Through the wall, I could hear the wireless next door playing dance music. I went outside to the toilet. When I come back I could see next door's curtains weren't drawn. The music was so loud you could hear it out there. A little boy about... I don't know. Must have been about... I could see him in the room dancing to the music, all by himself, like a little girl. No, not like a little girl, he was just like a little boy. I watched him in the cold. It was too.

In the second half of the play, he attributes this hypnotising figure, locating the source of all his love in Gerard:

> Vincent: You did for me, you know.
> Mrs Driscoll: Vincent.
> Gerard: What?
> Vincent: You did, you know.
> Gerard: I did for you?
> Mrs Driscoll: Vincent.
> Gerard: I. I did for you? I did?
> Mrs Harte: Gerard.
> Gerard: I did for you?
> Mrs Harte: Gerard.
> Gerard: I did?
> Mrs Harte: Gerard.

Vincent: You did, you know.
Mrs Driscoll: Vincent.
Gerard: I did?

It is Gerard who then claims to have been the dancing boy, something Vincent claims is impossible – the memory becomes contested and uncertain, as both make different claims for when and where it happened. But Vincent's overall claim is clear – it is because of Gerard that he is 'done for'.

Mrs Driscoll, meanwhile, a heartbreaking portrait of a broken woman, locates the source of all her love in a body that does not appear on the stage. Mrs Driscoll, like Mrs Shannon, is prone to fits of nerves:

Mrs Driscoll: I feel really bad. I'm in the middle of black-
leading the grate. I can't even work it off. He can be
so nice when he wants. He was out till gone quarter
to twelve last night.

These appear to be brought on by her husband, who is an uncaring drunk:

Mrs Driscoll: It's no good, I can't go to sleep if I'm in bed
on my own. And then when he's in that state I can't
go to sleep either.

The reason for these nerves, pathetically simple and commonplace, bursts out of Mrs Driscoll in one of the scenes she shares with Mrs Harte, visiting her neighbour in a moment of panic:

Mrs Driscoll: Oh, Mrs Harte, I wish he loved me.

Mrs Driscoll is a loveless woman, apparently still in love, and taking the failures of her marriage on herself:

Mrs Driscoll: Honestly, Mrs Harte, I wish I could pack it
all in... It's all my fault. It's my fault. I think it's my

fault, see?

It is this unhappiness, at the source of her larger nervous collapse, which eventually leads her to take her own life.

The larger, overwhelming unhappiness she feels is manifested in other characters, as in other Gill plays, as a kind of boredom and a desperation that grows from that:

> Gerard: Look at it.
> Mrs Harte: What?
> Gerard: All of it. In here. Out there. The street. I'm fed up. I'm fed up.
> Mrs Harte: You're fed up. That's a laugh. You're bloody fed up. A kid of your age. I'm fed up to the back teeth, I am.
> Gerard: And I'm bored.
> Mrs Harte: Bored. What you bored with then? Eh? Eh?
> Gerard: Oh, nothing, nothing. I'm going.

However, unlike other Gill plays, and unlike Mrs Driscoll, the other characters in *Small Change* direct their efforts to challenging this helplessness. The characters seek to express their problem, to develop a statement that can embrace and challenge their lives, and they pursue this expression in political as well as more abstract, philosophical terms. The greater political eloquence in the play is seen in exchanges between Vincent and Mrs Driscoll about the conditions of Vincent's apprenticeship:

> Vincent: What? It's not a fiddle, you keeping me on practically nothing for seven years, while they get free labour and skilled work, and then a skilled man at the end of it?

Mrs Driscoll tries to quieten these complaints:

> Mrs Driscoll: Bloody Catholics with your religion and your Labour party. You're all voice.

But this is not a play about silence, it is an attempt to put a situation into words, and Vincent refuses to follow his mother's example: 'I'm not just talking. I'm packing it in.' Gerard speaks of a coming revolution:

> Gerard: Do you know, where I am they think it's going to come from you...
> Vincent: They don't think I'm going to do anything, do they?

Gerard and Vincent share a long scene in the play's second half in which a political restlessness is circled and confronted, where the language of Gill's characters is able to accommodate ideas of injustice and imbalance that were previously only present in his work by implication, as when Gerard tells Vincent that 'Every piece of ugliness you see is... connected with an immense cruelty.' Gerard attempts to incite Vincent into some kind of action: 'You're covered in psychic fat. Psychic rind. Wrongs. Wrongs. Actual wrongs. Unnecessary sufferings that incapacitate any ability in you to change. For change. For all change.' Vincent still feels powerless to really change anything:

> Vincent: If everyone. You and me that is. If we were all to come out of our holes and put our shoulders to the wheel and say, now look, stop this, this isn't nice calling people old age pensioners and the like. And put our shoulders to the wheel. You see I don't trust your judgement. You could be putting your shoulder to the wrong wheel.

But simply to speak about these problems, where Jeffry and Dennis did not have the words, is a striking development for Gill's characters.

It is also, however, only part of the surface exchanges making up the play, rather than being the material the play is written out of. These political engagements are primarily surface traces of a larger attempt that is being made – the attempt to put a life into words, which has political implications and inevitably impacts on the political sphere, leading to the new engagement sketched above, but which is at its heart a personal struggle, located in the individual and the ties between him and what he loves, as Gerard reminds us when he tells his mother, 'you're all I have' – as all the characters remind us when they locate their love in other people, rather than in abstracts or ideas. In Gill's work, politics comes from humanity and develops from emotion, never the other way round. These faltering attempts to give expression to a thought occur as failures of speech throughout the play. Gerard and Vincent conduct wordless, attempted conversations:

> Gerard Did you...
> Vincent: Do you...
> Gerard: Was it... were you... did we...
> Vincent: When you... When I...
> Gerard: Were you... Did you... [He opens his mouth to
> speak again but can't].
>
> Vincent: Speak up.

Gerard focuses his energy on his mother, a woman who may already have died, who he may be re-animating as he tries, hopelessly, to change a life that has ended: 'You've got to change. Damn it all, you've got to stop. You've got to leave me alone.' He struggles because he is sure that in his relationship with his mother is the heart of his problem.

> Gerard: Stop now. Now. Now. Let's get it straight. Now.
> Now.
> Mrs Harte: I'm bad, Gerard.
> Gerard: I don't care. You mustn't. You're not.
> Mrs Harte: I'll have to sit down.
> Gerard: What are you doing? Tell me what is it? What is
> it? What is it?
> Mrs Driscoll: It's all right. I'll be out in a minute.
> Gerard: This is unfinished. This can't finish.
> Vincent: Mammy.
> *During the last lines H and D are knocked to the floor.*

The intense, repeated 'what is it? What is it? What is it?', echoing earlier failed questions, gets him nowhere – but he is compelled to revisit the question, to ask it again and again. This same revisiting seems to be taking place in Gerard's long exchange with Vincent, when he tries to recapture a perfect moment between them:

> Gerard: You said you loved me, then after we went to the
>   pictures. And then lying in bed, staying in your house
>   for a change., the kids asleep in the other corner, and
>   the light outside, whispering and talking and talking.

All of these are attempts to answer a question Gerard has posed earlier: 'What is it, what is it that will, will find the moment, that will...' The looping, doomed pursuit of an answer leads him, at the close of the play, to a gnomic Beckettian conclusion: 'Try but can't. Won't but can. Will but can't. Shall but don't.' The failure built into these repetitive half-sentences, and the fact that we hear him formulating oppositions again and again, organised and punctuated by the 'but' that foils each imperative, sees him unresolved at the play's close, unable to reconcile anything.

Part of the source of this futility may lie in the fact that Gerard is not, in fact, asking questions to which there is an answer any more, but re-animating disappeared voices, old arguments, vanished lives. Mrs Driscoll, a ghost on the stage once we know her suicidal fate, seems to show some self-knowledge of her status as memory rather than living being when she says this of Vincent:

> Mrs Driscoll: He's grieving. I'd come if I could. He's
>   grieving. He's never been a scrap of trouble to me,
>   and I'd love to help him. I'd get out of this if I could.
>   It's my fault I know. I'd come if I could.

The same retrospective tone is deployed for Mrs Harte later in the play, and the possibility surfaces that what we are watching is a series of re-animated ghosts, aware they are replaying an old tune, able to comment on how it went the first time:

> Mrs Harte: I watched it. I would have helped had it been possible... But I watched from a good seat going through much the same thing myself.

Gerard gestures towards the same idea himself:

> Gerard: In her hospital ward. The sadism of a hospital death. Making the dying cough up their lives.

The suggestion that these women have died and are never living in the play's 'present tense', which seems to be located finally in the long scene between Vincent and Gerard when they speak about pubs, politics and the past, makes all Gerard's attempts to engage with his mother futile. They are one-sided conversations, orderings of material that cannot actually be changed or explained, having already happened. For a moment, the suggestion even crosses the stage that none of this is living experience: that all of these characters are reliving lost experience. Gerard has an oblique speech about 'his' hospital:

> Gerard: In my hospital pain draws attention to the terminal case. All day he's fluttered his arms, let his blackened arms drift in the air... The three lamps in the ceiling are burning with dry ice. The sun is hanging under the old man's bed. The three white lamps are the three moons of the ward. The ward is tropical now and full of difficult beasts. The white globes flood red for night and we can't sleep.

It seems unlikely that *Small Change* is entirely a ghost play, but that 'we can't sleep' stands out, the collective term uniting these unquiet figures in an act of recollection and reconstitution.

Remembering, then, is at the heart of *Small Change*. It is a play about this activity, the attempt to change something in the memory, the impossibility of doing so. Gerard admits to re-animating old stories:

> Gerard: But who am I keeping alive with my actions? Why

doesn't somebody put me down? Kill her by killing
me.

He knows he has become locked in the past, far from the
'actual present':

> Gerard: If you've got out of the habit of living in the
> present... If the past's out of perspective. If the
> past's... If you've got out of – See... If the past's... In
> the past sometimes you can locate pain and feel safe
> in its hurt – it having gone. If it's bearable you're all
> right, but if it's not and the past was not, the attempt
> to make a bearable present is made hopeless by
> keeping faith with the moral horrors of the past.

This leads Vincent to comment, 'you've got a war memorial
mentality', and later to add 'there you go, you see, you won't live,
will you?' That memorialising, though, is unsatisfactory to
Gerard. Creating an image, a photograph, does not do justice to
the story he is trying to capture:

> Gerard: It's not only pictures of the past that invented me,
> but the literal past.

What he realises he is trying to put into words is his whole life.
The moment he is trying to locate is his entire experience, as it
was his mother's whole life that constituted the moment that 'did
for her':

> Gerard: There are more ways of doing it than pills and
> drink or banister and rope or downing caustic. Some
> people do it very slowly over the years.

But there is another, hidden subject behind this, almost a
subconscious influence, that renders this attempt at life as
memory only a symptom, rather than a cause, of the play. Each
character, as we have seen, is structured by reference to the
source of their love, the person or location where they decided to

focus their care. In all of these exchanges, the deafening silence is the one surrounding fathers. Vincent's is spoken about, as a drunk, a traveller, a distant figure who drives Mrs Driscoll to suicide. Gerard's seems absent entirely. The two men only engage with these absences in their lives at the end of acts one and two of the play:

> Vincent: Dear Daddy, I hope you are well, that you are in good health and that it's all right where you are. Dear Daddy, I wish you were home. Dear Daddy, I wish you could come home for good. I hope I'll get another postcard again. We all got our cards and we hope you got ours. Lots of love, your son till death – John Vincent O'Driscoll.

> Gerard: In the other photograph, there's a deck chair, with some children piled into it. All in white. Standing behind them, leaning on the back of the deckchair is a man. He's quite vivid really. Dressed in white. Hair brushed back. White trousers and shirt with sleeves rolled back to the elbow and white sleeveless pullover and a dark tie. He's graceful, giving the impression of being tall. Like a cricketer, with graceful arms and hands and legs.

These speeches are Gill at his allusive and moving best. After all the noise about politics, about love, about memory, it is revealed to us as the lights come back up that all the activity has been an attempt to treat another absence, far more painful, far too difficult to approach directly. They have been a way of circling the absent fathers at the heart of the play. The suggestion is plain enough in the tone of Vincent's postcard, and Gerard's loving description of this white, angelic figure, as inscrutable in his pristine description as the bundle of the self with which we began this reading, that it is here that both men feel all their love has been tied up and kept from them. It is these men who have 'done for' their mothers, and their investigations of the deaths of their mothers, women they knew and could understand, were attempts to engage with this absence, this lack of love, through something they could understand, and had experienced themselves. Gill's play has seemed to be all about speaking, but really its subject, once again, was silence, and avoiding the subject, circling and existing in the shadow of an idea as a way of engaging with something too difficult and painful to be effectively spoken about directly. Wittgenstein's famous dictum, 'that of which we cannot speak, we must pass over in silence', is observed here, after a fashion. Except that what Gill studies is the impact of speechlessness, when the unspeakable subject is what organises the lives of individuals.

5. EXPLORATIONS
RIVERSIDE STUDIOS, *KICK FOR TOUCH, IN THE BLUE,*
MEAN TEARS

For forty years, more or less from the time of his arrival in London, Gill lived in a house in Hammersmith which has strong claim to being one of the most interesting theatrical footnotes of the postwar British theatre. He came to move in there shortly after taking up his first job as an Assistant Stage Manager at the Lyric Hammersmith – but to tell the story from its beginning, it is necessary to detour briefly to Oxford in the 1930s.

George Devine became President of the Oxford University Dramatic Society, or OUDS, in 1931. He had developed an interest in theatre while at school which intensified while he read for a degree in history at Wadham, but it was as President of OUDS that he first had an opportunity to display his entrepreneurial flair as a producer.

His master-stroke was to engage John Gielgud, then a young star actor, to direct the OUDS in a production of *Romeo and Juliet*. By proxy, he also therefore engaged Gielgud's address book: Gielgud brought Edith Evans and Peggy Ashcroft with him to join the acting company (women were not admitted to OUDS at this time) and insisted the production was designed by Motley, then a newly formed trio of stage designers who would go on to make an immense contribution to shaping the aesthetic of the twentieth century British theatre. Their names were Elizabeth Montgomery, Margaret 'Percy' Harris and Sophie Harris. As well as being the catalyst for Devine's career (he never sat his Finals, moving to London to become an actor instead), the production had a profound effect on his personal life, as he began a relationship with the third of these designers, Sophie Harris, that would lead to marriage ten years later and last thirty years.

By the time Peter Gill came to London, this marriage had ended, and Devine was living with Jocelyn Herbert. Sophie Harris and her daughter Harriet Devine were living in a house in Lower Mall in Hammersmith, and Harriet, a student at LAMDA, met Gill and suggested he move in with them. Gill joined a coterie of lodgers which included, over the years, Tony Richardson and Nicholas Wright, and while he lived there the house acted as a centre for the social lives of two decades of Royal Court directors. It was at dinner there that Gill first met William Gaskill, the director who would act as mentor to his early career, and Gill himself is well remembered by visitors to the house for organising complicated parlour games after dinner.

The history of this house is fascinating because I think it gives those of us attempting to understand the phenomenon of the Royal Court after the fact access to a vital secret about its success. When I began researching this book, I wanted among other things to find out a little more about why the Royal Court had achieved what it did during the time Gill was most closely associated with it: why the theatre in this country had so suddenly and emphatically become interesting. I heard many answers in the course of many interviews – resoundingly, that the Court was a theatre that prioritised the writer and sought to encourage serious writers back onto the stage, and in prioritising that goal where no other theatre had in recent memory, inevitably made some progress; that the insistence on fidelity to the play as delivered by the writer had a profound effect; that the introduction of French ideas from George Devine and the ideas of the Berliner Ensemble, primarily from Bill Gaskill, transformed the landscape; that the war made that kind of revitalisation of ideas inevitable; that the Court had been above all an actor's theatre, and that the sustained support of particular, extraordinary actors had led to particular, extraordinary results; that the Court was in fact a director's theatre, a collection of the most brilliant theatre directors of their generation all being astutely recruited and retained and given free reign or something like it on the theatre's two stages; that there was a sensuality to the work of the Court which marked it out from anything before or since. Once again,

I ran up against the more direct pragmatism that is at the heart of Gill's work – the key tenet of the Court at that time seemed to me to lie in Bill Gaskill's observation when once questioned on artistic policy that 'policy is the people you work with'. But none of these quite satisfied – they were all self-evidently true, after all, even where they were self-contradictory (a theatre, being numerous people under one banner, is never just one thing). None of them had the look of a secret ingredient.

It was through hearing the stories of Harriet Devine's house on Lower Mall that I felt I had happened upon the secret of the Court during that period: that it was a family before it was anything else. Almost everyone closely involved in the Court from the 60s through to the 80s spent evenings at this house – and long after George Devine himself had died, therefore, people were still meeting for dinner in the house he had lived in, continuing to live not just in his artistic but also his social and cultural shadow. Bearing in mind the extraordinary consistency of purpose and achievement at the Court during this period, this seems of some relevance to me. Gaskill had gestured towards the idea with his comment about artistic policy, but had not quite revealed what the policy of the Court had been, who the people he worked with were and where they were drawn from. Gill first worked at the Court through meeting Gaskill at dinner, not in an interview; it was a theatre united by sensibility, conversation, shared emotional as well as artistic bonds.

It is a widely held and sensible view that a group of people with shared sensibilities and complementary talents will make steadily richer work together as they collaborate on project after project, and the body of shared experience and collective frame of reference expands between them with each new show. In Europe, where companies stay together for decades, this is the basis of working practise. In Britain, the conditions do not exist to make this kind of work a priority, and directors must go around keeping their permanent companies in their heads, ready to be called on when the parts arise, if they happen to believe in this particular philosophy of collaborative working – but wherever the idea of a genuine collective, a group of people committed to each other in the longer term, has been given time and resources, the results have invariably been interesting. The Royal Court of this period seems to me, read through the cipher of Harriet Devine's house on Lower Mall, to have been another collective; and this seems to me to be a persuasive factor in the theatre's continuity and success.

Through living on Lower Mall Gill came to found Riverside Studios. As he tells it, the Riverside project came about almost by accident. A set of BBC television studios on the riverfront was being closed, and a group of local people from the arts and business were corralled to have some oversight of the future of the building – Gill, being local, joined the board. Rather than demolish the building or sell it off, Gill argued for a local arts centre – and because no one seemed particularly clear on what kind of arts centre might work there, he then volunteered to organise a festival of work. The festival, which featured a revival of his recent Royal Court production of *Small Change*, was a success, and Gill was appointed as the artistic director of Riverside Studios, a venue initially organised around festivals which expanded while he ran it to host a year-round programme across the arts.

Riverside became, under Gill's leadership, an extraordinary success – it is difficult to imagine a building opening today that could so quickly establish such a vital role in our culture. Gill proved an astute programmer. Plays designed by Joan Miro or directed by Tadeusz Kantor or written by Athol Fugard played there; Joint Stock and Samuel Beckett (Gill used to pass him in the corridor, but was too shy to say hello) presented their work. Exhibitions for the front of house area were astutely selected, with early breaks given to Howard Hodgkin among others, and Gill's search for interesting people to fill his building filtered through every level of the theatre – Daniel Mornin and Hanif Kureishi ran the bookshop in the foyer. Gill's flair as a programmer ensured that Riverside developed seemingly irresistibly into an arts centre that offered the very best of national and international work to Hammersmith and, more widely, all of London. He also used his position to develop his own work as a director, working with larger companies to produce a sequence of productions that were to lead to his employment at the National Theatre, re-affirming the reputation he had established with the Lawrence plays as a director of extraordinary precision and feeling. In the brief spell from 1977 to 1980 when he ran Riverside, Gill directed *The Cherry Orchard, The Changeling, Measure for Measure, Julius Caesar* and *Scrape off the Black* by Tunde Ikoli – a sustained engagement with the classic theatre that saw him taking full advantage of the resources available to him as Artistic Director of a successful venture, and the conditions he was able to create. *The Cherry Orchard* and *Julius Caesar*, in particular, are regarded as some of his finest work.

It would, after a fashion, be Gill's first production at Riverside following on from the revival of *Small Change* that would lead to his departure after four years to work at the National Theatre. Gill programmed *The Cherry Orchard* for a slot very close to a production of the same play Peter Hall was due to direct for the National Theatre. A call duly came from Hall, in which Gill was informed in no uncertain terms that 'we do not do this – when Trevor and I are doing plays we call each other first'. Hall was unhappy that two productions of *The Cherry Orchard* would be on in London more or less at once. Gill went ahead with his, receiving superlative reviews, and it is reasonable to suggest that from this time onwards Hall had his eye on Gill and his serial successes at Riverside, so that when a vacancy arose for an Associate Director at the National, Hall thought of Gill, and when he came to found a Studio for the National Theatre, he thought of Gill to run it – Gill's achievement in lassoing talent as he did at the Riverside proved the perfect audition for such a role.

This is not to say that Riverside should be read in any way as a long job application, or an accident Gill fell into. The years he spent there were the first time he was able to express his own personality through the work he programmed and the people he gathered around him, rather than be part of the personality of the Court, and in doing so with such success he marked himself out as an artist of taste and intelligence, whose uncompromising standards really did lead to extraordinary results. His run through a repertoire of classic plays was not the programming of someone attempting to prove themselves and catch the eyes of others, but someone who finally had the chance to direct whatever he wanted, to hone talents already discovered and developed in earlier projects at the Court and in America. Gill proved himself as a director and an artist through the conspicuous success of Riverside Studios – these years elevated him beyond the position he had held at the Court, and were to lead in due course to the successes of his mature career at the National Theatre. The years at Riverside seem also to have been the period when Gill moved from being a member of a Royal Court coterie to a director with a coterie of his own, a man at the centre of a movement. Since his years at the National Theatre Studio and through to the present day, Gill has been remarkable for the loyalty and passionate, intense admiration he has inspired in a band of collaborators and associates, a talent never put more succinctly than by Marjorie Yates when she told me, 'he's our God.' This tribal sense of affinity is rooted in the same kinds of shared sensibilities Gill experienced and was part of at his home in Lower Mall, though the tastes he honed with his collaborators at the Studio were to advance the tastes of that earlier coterie in a different direction. It is an extraordinary achievement for someone who began life where he did to be able to express his talent in such a way as to be recognised as an artist worth rallying round – social mobility was greater when he was growing up than it is today, but his achievement is nonetheless profound. It was through his work at Riverside Studios that he began doing this.

★

Kick for Touch was first produced, in repertory with *Small Change*, on the Cottesloe stage of the National Theatre, London, on 15 February 1983, with the following cast:

Joe – Kenneth Cranham
Jim – James Hazeldene
Eileen – Jane Lapotaire

Directed by Peter Gill

Kick for Touch is an oblique portrayal of three people whose lives are inextricably entwined, where nothing is made immediately clear to its audience, who attend the play as eavesdroppers on scenes that overlap each other, not in chronological order, without concession to an outsider's narrative understanding of the story. A portrait of the three characters – Joe, Jim and Eileen – builds up subtly through the different scenes, as the audience is drip fed pieces of information, slowly developing them into the whole world of the play. But one of the most telling images of the play is the one that begins it – while Joe and Jim talk around a kitchen table, Eileen sits with her back to the auditorium, detached from the action around her and the audience in the room. This disconnection, and the distance it places between characters and audience, words and meaning, is at the centre of the play.

At first, the play seems to be a restatement of the character types already found in *Over Gardens Out* and *Small Change* – Joe, returning home to Cardiff, comes to visit Jim, letting himself in by the back door. Jim draws the parallel plainly when he says to Joe: 'You don't alter much, do you?' Small change here, then, and the observation also restates material developed in previous work: Joe replies, 'What's there to alter me?', and it is clear we are revisiting a world of absence and emptiness we know from Gill's earlier plays, where young men are directionless, when the working class experience no meaningful changes in their frustrated lives. Halfway through the play the spectre of the big world, of television and celebrity and success crosses the stage, as it does in *Over Gardens Out* under the flickering light of the televisions, as Joe entertains himself by singing Elvis and Jim by quoting Marlon Brando and James Dean, culminating in the 'contender' speech from *On The Waterfront*. This brief inhabiting of the lives of idols, the most beautiful and iconic men in the world, is of course an ordinary activity, no different to singing in the shower or modern karaoke television, but it puts the lives of these characters in a context that casts an overwhelming shadow on their lives, diminishes them by contrast and defines their aspirations and their own escapism, which is the basis of their culture and indeed of much culture, as they imagine brighter lives than theirs. As in previous plays, the two men struggle to speak honestly with each other across the distances established in the play through geography and time, and through the extent to which they are not the people they dream of being. On this occasion, they opt for the male staple of finding solace in football, turning metronomically to discussion of sport when they have nothing else to say:

> Jim: [*After a pause.*] Did you play on Saturday?
> Joe: Aye, I had a game.
> Jim: Wonder they let you play, an old man like you.
> [*Then it breaks down and after a pause...*]
> Joe: I had a game of rugby the week before last.

These shield conversations are surely familiar to any father or son – moments when sport fills the silence between two people, both of whom are uncomfortably aware as they speak that they are not actually talking, not really connecting, just batting a ball of well-worn words back and forth.

These points of departure, then, are familiar ground for Gill, and it is difficult, coming across an apparently close re-imagination of the *Over Gardens Out/Small Change* relationship, not to recall Beckett's description of *Mercier and Camier* as the 'grisly afterbirth' of his Trilogy, and wonder whether *Kick for Touch* is more than an extension of previous ideas. However, it is the way those ideas are developed that sets *Kick for Touch* apart, the unique variations of the play's exchanges evolving a complex and confounding picture. Gill's own metaphor for his creative process is of a play as a coagulation of ideas, but in reading *Kick for Touch*, another reading of what the plays are and what they are doing suggests itself. *Kick for Touch*'s musical and complex variations on recognisable preoccupations offer us a theatre as kaleidoscope, an image of Gill's plays as successive looks into the same interior that result in radically different patterns emerging from the material of the subconscious. It is as if with each play, Gill opens a window into his imagination, and we glimpse the current phase of an ongoing, churning digestion of life, the current form he has given to his experience of his life, like watching the different shapes smoke takes, as memory continually recedes down the conveyor belt of the mind into imagination.

It becomes rapidly clear that there is some greater fracture between Jim and Joe than previous Gill pairs have experienced: where Vincent and Gerard fill the second half of *Small Change* with a reunion, Joe appears to have avoided one with Jim:

> Joe: I was up your way.
> Jim: When?
> Joe: Ooo... fortnight ago it must be.
> Jim: Why didn't you call in?
> Joe: I should have.
> Jim: Why didn't you?
> Joe: I will next time.
> Jim: Oh yeah.

The regret implicit in Joe's 'I should have', whether honest or feigned, a turn of speech or a careful phrasing, opens the way to a discovery of a vast, fraught past between the two men, that begins to show as Gill's scene fragments, slipping from one conversation to another, and forcing speech from the still invisible Eileen:

> Jim: You going out?
> Joe: Well, I was going out.
> Jim: Well, don't stop me.
> Joe: No, I won't.
> Eileen: Don't go out.

What is the competition that causes this needling, and why does Eileen speak up about it? This slightly combative note continues as Jim questions Joe about his giro:

> Jim: Have you signed on?
> Joe: What?
> Jim: Don't get shirty. I'm only asking. Have you?
> Joe: Of course I have.

Jim: Have you?
Joe: Of course I have.

Jim finishes this exchange by saying, 'I knew you hadn't signed on', though Joe only concedes the point by not replying. Again, Joe's resistance to Jim, and Jim's pursuit of Joe seems unexplained, the surface evidence of some problem we must get to by increments, that the play must find a way to express.

The problem the play works towards reveals itself slowly, and is never stated outright, but the situation that emerges through the action of the play is a complex triangle between Jim, Joe and Eileen. This relationship is characterised by deep need and deep antipathy, in equal and contradictory measure. Eileen reaches out to Jim one moment, only to reject him the next:

Eileen: Please, Jim. Jimmy. Let me come back with you.
    Please.
Jim: I can't, love. How can I?

This is followed by a reversal of roles:

Jim [*To Eileen*]: What is it? What's the matter? Tell me. Eh?
    Don't. Don't, love.
Eileen: Don't look at me, please.
Jim: Tell me. What is it?
Eileen: Don't look at me. Please. Please, Jim, let me come
    back with you.

The characters cannot synchronise their emotions. The desire of one to be nearer another seems almost directly to cause the other to put distance between them, to continue to isolate themselves. What the characters themselves diagnose is a hopeless lack of understanding, of sympathy between each other:

Jim: She told me you didn't understand her. That you
    never really understood her.
Joe: She really didn't understand me.
Jim: I don't understand you.

> Joe: What's there to understand? I'm straightforward
>   enough.
> Jim: She told me she didn't understand you either.
> Joe: Oh, did she? Well, we were made for each other then,
>   weren't we?

Just as important to the nature of these relationships is how angry Joe shows himself to be in his reaction to Jim's final accusation. The inability and the need to understand or express emotion go hand in hand in these interactions:

> Joe: Did she say anything about me?
> Jim: Nothing at all.
> Joe: Nothing at all?
> Jim: Nothing at all.

Joe, speaking of Eileen's boy, expresses in the memory of an action the overwhelming, physical urge of love motivating him:

> Joe [*Of the boy outside*]: When he was asleep at first used
>   to wake him. Hold a mirror to his mouth... I have to
>   stop myself sometimes holding on to him.

But this loved object is not present on the stage; he is an eloquent absence, a set of clothes being cleaned, a memory, viewed across a distance:

> Joe: Once I thought I saw him going down the other
>   street, where the houses are being pulled down. There
>   was a door open into the house. I thought I saw his
>   mother, her sleeves rolled up, drying another boy by
>   the fire. Another boy, stronger-limbed than him.

As with other plays of Gill's, we see an adult struggling to engage with a child – where Jeffry thought a runny nose was a nosebleed, Joe thinks sleep is death, and remembers this boy as very far away and disappearing from his vision. Joe experiences the same distance between himself and his mother and father, who appear to have fostered him, in his memories of them, and turns to literary fantasy to fill an absence in his experience of family love:

> Joe: Sometimes they're together, sometimes single, or sometimes I'm under the currant bushes between the end of the garden and hers. Or sometimes she's down his end and they're pulling the line up in the wind. He always used to smoke his pipe outside... I used to pretend that I'd been with them much longer. Not that I'd been born there, mind you. But instead of being brought up on the bus and handed over that he'd brought me home one night unexpectedly when I was very little – carried me inside his overcoat.

Whether or not he knows he slips into picturing himself as Heathcliff, what is clear is that the only physical sensation attached to this memory is a substitute for real experience – an imagined feeling that is a way of filling a space. The overriding action of this act of imagining, therefore, is to reveal the space and absence Joe perceives, rather than actually to fill it. Finally, the characters observe the same distance between themselves as well, that has been forced on them by past events:

> Joe: What did she want to do that for? Eh? What did you want to leave us for?
> Jim: You left me.
> Joe: I didn't.
> Jim: Didn't you?

Everyone knows something has gone, but no one can agree on what it was.

Thickening this difficult mixture is the suggestion that Jim and Joe are brothers, a factor which renders the fraught three-way relationship indissoluble. Rifts exist between them which are common between brothers:

> Jim: He thinks I had it better than him. I think he had it

> better than me. You see?
> E: No.
> Jim: I can't forgive him for taking so long to like me. For
>   taking so long to forgive me. I hate him for that. I do.
>   I don't think he ever liked me. I don't think I like him.
>   I think really I don't like you.

The family connection, as is so often the case, is also a family divide, and that contradiction also enters into both men's relationships with Eileen, whose bond to them seems just as strong.

The other problem which overshadows the play is the presence of children. During the play we learn that Eileen is uncertain who the father of her first child is. She then has a second child, and the play ends with her leading these two boys onto the stage, younger mirror images of Joe and Jim, who by this point are lying on the floor, invisible to Eileen. She ends the play by asking 'where are you both?', her two boys standing beside her, and the final impression is that the slipping, intertwining conversations animated for us on the stage have faded from her view, silenced by the image of these two young boys.

What dominates *Kick for Touch* is a profound sense of loss – of problems which are unsolvable and desires which are unobtainable, for the simple fact that their origin or solution lies in the past, a time that is lost to the characters and an idea of their lives that was never quite realised, and now haunts their present, day-to-day existences. Joe relays to Jim at one point in the play a speech given to him by one of a queue of wrecked men in the local job centre: 'you only die one time he said. You don't die twice. You only die one time. You don't see daylight no more. We've all got to go, haven't we, he said. I've got six months to live.' What the play suggests is slightly different to this – we see these characters dying many times, as the scenes of their lives surface and disappear before us. The world is constantly vanishing around them, as they observe themselves:

> Joe: Anyway, what's the point of going in for this house?
>   They're clearing all this eventually.

Eileen, Joe and Jim are left uncertain and beached among memories in what is left of the world around them:

> Eileen: Everything I was brought up to believe in has gone. There's no heaven and no God. And if there was I'm sure I'm not fit to meet them.

This uncertainty is paralysing for Eileen, who shows herself to be trapped and afraid in her own life, which she cannot take control of:

> Eileen: I was frightened.
> Jim: What of?
> Eileen: Of what might happen. Of what could happen.
> Jim: What could happen?
> Eileen: I don't know.

Joe's accusation seems to speak to the condition of all the characters when he says, 'You're not sure, are you? That's what it is.' None of them are sure about themselves or their lives:

> Jim: You wonder what it is about you that made them do it. That's what it amounts to. What it is about you. What it is about you that made it happen. It was bad at one time. The feeling. Very bad... You know it's not you. But all the same you feel that it must be. Mm mm mm. You. Well, you found a way.

The only suggestion of comprehension of their lives, of cohesion and calm in their lives, lies in the past – in the silencing stage gesture of the two boys entering the stage, blank canvasses, the image of what has been lost and the result of the confusions of the lives of the three main protagonists. Joe's last words to Jim are 'Oh kid. When you were little. When you were little.' Moments later, the children enter the stage, and it appears that all the confusion and difficulty of this haunting and complex play have been the absences at the heart of these characters, who are each similarly heartbroken, unable to express a lost past, a disappeared earlier time that they did not realise was perfect as it happened but now believe must have been so.

Kick for Touch is perhaps Gill's most complex play to date, the high watermark of his invention and obliquity. It is therefore the best expression of the value of Gill's theatre to our own lives, because I believe Gill's unique achievement lies in his formal innovations. Many of Gill's colleagues speak of his 2001 play *The York Realist*, which I will address in a later chapter, as his greatest achievement. It is a relatively formally conventional, well made play – relatively, not formulaically, but set against a play like *Kick for Touch* it is certainly a strikingly simply told tale. Upon seeing the production, many of his colleagues told me they wondered how many other well-made plays might have been suppressed over the years in pursuit of a more fragmented narrative structure. It fell to Michael Grandage to rebut any sense of regret that between *The Sleepers Den* and *The York Realist*, Gill did not tell a story in a conventional, naturalistic way. Grandage's eloquent analysis of Gill's work was that his plays are fragmented because we do not experience life as a well-made play. We experience life as a collage of impressions, inflected and reorganised always by memory, new experiences always conditional upon and prompting reflection on former experiences. We experience life as a mess, as a dance between multiple time signatures, as an ebb-tide always pulling us away from the present and into the past. A well-made play, in that sense, is far less naturalistic than Gill's creative organisation of material: the value of a well-made play is that it shapes and structures life into something simpler, more focused and driven than it actually is, in doing so presenting us with an easily interpreted portrait. But life, as every philosopher and theologian ever to think or write will attest, is far from being that. Gill's importance, then, lies in his refusal to treat theatre as a form of simplified life. His work is a rendering of the complexity of experiencing consciousness. Few other writers engage at all with this subject, so Gill's sustained meditation on the difficulty of reconciling the human urge to find meaning and narrative in the world – because, I suppose, we are conditioned by the fact that time passes and our bodies age in chronological order to attempt to think in a linear fashion – with the fact that the world does not have a meaning, but is simply event after event prompting reflections on other events and allowing us to exist simultaneously in the present and the past, in our bodies and our minds, marks him out as a uniquely serious thinker in the theatre.

It has been my suspicion from the beginning of my own career that the theatre has to work very hard not to fall into being an unambitious trade. Before I had a job in the theatre, I went on a writing course for new playwrights, where the course leader, whenever he spoke about inspiration and starting to tell a new story, would ask – 'what makes you angry?' This editorial slant on creativity was never interrogated in the course, but a couple of years later, in a poetry workshop with a prominent American writer, I did get a partial explanation when the poet told us, 'write about what makes you angry, because anger's the strongest emotion to write out of.' This struck me first of all as a sad insight into the emotional life of that particular poet, but as it was also something I had heard being taught as gospel at a leading theatre writing programme, I felt it had further, more provocative implications.

A theatre which only sets out to interrogate one section of the emotional spectrum experienced by human beings is surely, logically going to struggle to be of more than partial relevance to the society it seeks to reflect: it will never be able to hold more than a fragment of a mirror up to nature. And a theatre which generates its new material from within the relatively narrow emotional context of a play written more than fifty years ago – epoch-making as *Look Back In Anger* was – is surely, logically always going to run the risk of falling into the same unimaginative cycle of rehearsal and production John Osborne sought to reinvigorate. If playwrights are encouraged to write out of a particular, narrow sphere of experience, then the theatre is at some level encouraging the constant reiteration of a formula as tried, tested, commercially driven and philosophically and ideologically unimaginative as the bourgeois theatre its patron saint, Jimmy Porter, was once celebrated for shaking up.

The first thing to say, of course, is that much theatre makes no secret of being a commercially driven product; that one of the primary functions of the theatre, to entertain, whatever that means, is not badly served by the honing of certain particularly successful formulae; and that the world of petrolheads and trainspotters proves mankind has a deep-seated interest in observing well-built machines at work, which is well served by watching, say, a farce or a musical. The second thing to say is that it is not the case, and never has been, that all contemporary theatre writing is done out of anger. But the battle against homogeny in the theatre is not fought loudly enough: while theatres such as the Young Vic make active attempts to send young artists abroad and immerse them in different theatre cultures, not much is done to counter the fact that the majority of young writers trying to make a name for themselves are best advised to move to London, get a part time job and start chiselling away at the big new writing rock faces until they make themselves a foothold. The result of this is that most young writers are living very similar lives, in similar places, on similar incomes, drinking in similar bars and speaking in similar idioms, aspiring to interest the same literary managers or agents who will, of course, have certain tastes and values which young writers will seek to satisfy through the way they write and the things they write about. This isn't all bad – the theatre's an innately urbanising pastime because its job is to gather people together to share an experience in the same place at the same time, so a preoccupation with life in the modern, urban world is a vital subject, being the experience most theatre audiences are going to be most concerned with. However, there are more things in heaven and earth than are dreamt of in such a philosophy, so schemes such as the Pearson Playwright programme, that assigns writers to regional theatres for a time, and the theatres around the country that commit to generating new plays, such as Plymouth Theatre Royal or Newcastle Live, therefore seem vital in nurturing a genuinely diverse discourse in the new writing theatre. The existence of a writer like Gill is also of importance to a challenge such as this. Gill's work is interested in more than what makes him angry. It interrogates sorrow and memory and love, belief and doubt, hope and mourning; it shows us working class Cardiff and gay London; it lifts stones unturned elsewhere in the theatre, and sets a vital example in doing so.

This lifting of stones is at the centre of my reading of the social function of a theatre. The theatre seems to me to serve a valuable function when it acts as a focus for and an expression of the community it serves; when it provides people with a chance to go out for an evening (one thinks of Larkin's 'MCMXIV' when he writes of 'thousands of marriages, / Lasting a little while longer', which is to rob that line of much of its poignancy, but which I believe is relevant in a discussion of what the theatre is for at a more pragmatic level than what it does on the stage), and when it prompts thought and reminds audiences how very big the world is. For it to do that effectively, it must reach further than anger and the urban experience. Folk musicians are the artists I have encountered who seem to have the clearest sense of social function: their job is to go out into the hedgerows, collect the stories buried there, and bring them back for the big world to look at, in order to encourage them to examine their own lives. A play like *Kick for Touch* is important because its author has gone very far off the beaten track, and brought back a story we would not otherwise have heard.

*

In the Blue was first performed at a Studio Night in the Cottesloe auditorium of the National Theatre on 18 March 1985, and subsequently was included as part of the National Theatre Studio's Festival of New Plays at the Cottesloe in November 1985, with the following cast:

Stewart – Ewan Stewart
Michael – Michael Maloney

Directed by Peter Gill
Designed by Alison Chitty
Lighting designed by Laurence Clayton

★

In the Blue is a departure from Gill's earlier plays, in that it is the first original play he wrote that was not set in Cardiff. This unmooring from the sense and exploration of place that had dominated earlier plays is emphasised by the setting of this piece: it takes places in a set described as the 'suggestion of a room' – a few books on the floor, a few clothes, no furniture. Gill's plays had always explored dislocation and alienation, but within a specific, perhaps paradoxically rooted context. With *In the Blue*, for the first time, his characters are very much floating in the space that is also the play's subject – the space between the two characters, Michael and Stewart.

There is still, of course, a society around Michael and Stewart, the play's two protagonists, that is visible in their actions, informing their behaviour. The world they inhabit is London, specifically a London populated by rent boys (Michael suggests Stewart should charge, as he has the kind of flat and lives on the kind of street where people do) and down-and-outs. Stewart vividly portrays the world he is accustomed to when remembering a doss house he once stayed in:

> Stewart: I was in this doss in London and one morning I
> went to take a piss, and someone came in and said,
> where's Lenny and tried to kick the cubicle door in. So
> I went into the next cubicle and I pulled myself up to
> look about, and there he was, Lenny, sitting with his
> head rolled back and a needle beside him on the floor.
> Then the superintendent rang the police and said, he's
> dead as far as I can see. Take your time, anyway. He's
> no use to anyone. An old man died in the same doss,
> so the authorities came to take the body away. They
> handed him as far as te landing then one of them says
> 'Hey up' and tipped him over the banister. They never
> caught him. They put him in a box and carted him off.

These two horrific stories help situate the world that Gill is exposing to our attention in *In the Blue* – it is the world Orwell earlier explored in *Down and Out In Paris and London* as much as it is the London gay scene, a rundown environment, populated by forgotten and unloved people. These characters are trapped and isolated on their small islands within London:

> Michael: He says he's moving.
> Stewart: Where's he moving to?
> Michael: Tottenham.
> Stewart: That's nice. You'll be able to go for a holiday.

Like Jim and Joe in *Kick for Touch*, the drama in their lives is set into sad relief by contrasts with the big world, comparisons which don't seem likely to live up to their claims:

> Michael: He says the postcard looks like me.
> Stewart: Let's have a see. Who is it?
> Michael: Keats.

Unlike Keats, Michael and Stewart struggle to express themselves – they are, once again, a portrait of humanity wrestling with connection, with speech and sympathy. Their ineloquence, as they try to connect with one another, is painful:

> Stewart: Thank you for the...
> Michael: Oh, that's... listen, ring first, OK? Don't...
> Stewart: No.
> Michael: It might be...
> Stewart: Yeah.

This clumsiness is mirrored in a reticence, displayed here by Michael, to honestly express feelings:

> Michael: You're beautiful. I know that. Or... I thought of
> having my ears pierced.

The revision, as Michael seems to withdraw from the crisis he decides he does not have the strength to force, shows us a character who lives in an unrealised state, unable to fully express himself. He is ordinary, and human, and therefore struggles to speak. This emotional reticence is constant in the interactions of the two men, who hesitate to trust, to make contact:

> Michael: Or it could be... what is it?
> Stewart: I think I've got something in my eye.
> Michael: Come here.
> Stewart: No.

Michael's evasions go as far as to refuse to tell Stewart his own name:

> Stewart: What are you called?
> Michael: Stewart.
> Stewart: No. Come on. Come on.

Gill's play documents a failing relationship, but it does so through an extraordinary prism, showing us a series of exchanges and possible exchanges as imagined by Michael, who asks early in the play: 'I wonder if he'll ring. He might ring. He won't ring. Why would he ring? What if he rings?' That 'what if?' proceeds to animate the drama, as Michael hypothesises his way through his life with Stewart, showing the audience not quite what they had, but a number of possible variations of that life, refracted through memory and imagination. These refractions are triggered by Michael proposing an alternative scene which is then played out:

> Michael: Or...
> Stewart: Do you want to leave it then?
> Michael: If you want to.
> Stewart: Do you want to? Give me your number.
> Michael: Or perhaps...
> Stewart: Well... I'm off... I'll phone you... shall I?

Sometimes these will change the tack of the scene, and sometimes only the phrasing:

Michael: Or... do you want the number?
Stewart: No.
Michael: Or... do you want the number?
Stewart: No. Thanks.

They seem to document Michael's imagining of what might have been between the two men, as well as what actually was, a world he was too afraid to grasp and bring to life at the time it happened, which he now re-imagines ceaselessly, like the dreaming figure in Beckett's *But the clouds*, or the compulsive remembering in Gill's own *Small Change*. The 'or' device was developed during rehearsals of the play at the National Theatre Studio, as a method of cohering the fragments Gill had brought into the rehearsal room. *In the Blue* initially existed as a collection of short, fragmentary exchanges between the two characters, and Gill had no idea how they were going to be connected together. Collaborators on the project remember him coming into rehearsal one day with the 'or' device fully evolved, the problem of the fragments solved suddenly by the realisation that they had not woven themselves together into single scenes because they were not supposed to be played in such a way – the 'or' unlocked their actual, kaleidoscopic function.

The centre of this inability to connect, and of this play, is arrived at through the movement of the two characters through the scenes. Stewart tries to prompt it from Michael:

Michael: Or it could be... Then it could be... Or it could be...
Stewart: Do you want me to stay?
Michael: Or... it could be No. Or... No.
Stewart: What's the matter?
Michael: Or...
Stewart: What is it?
Michael: Or... No. Or...
Stewart: It's alright.
Michael: No.
Stewart: Come on. Come on. What's the matter?

The answer does not come at first, but lies buried in the detail. There is a tenderness between the characters that is the source of some of their reticence:

> Michael: Or...
> Stewart: I don't want to hurt you.

In addition to this, Michael's self-doubt seems to consume him, rendering him powerless, apparently obsessed with mortality and futility:

> Michael: How am I going to get through? A lot of people spend their lives just in drink... Don't have any afterwards. When you drop dead. Do you want everlasting life? Just got to grow old, when you come to think of it. Does that worry you? I think the problems start when you start listening to yourself.

But even this strong emotion cannot galvanise Michael – it embarrasses him instead. He describes it as overdramatic: 'If someone had died I'd have some reason for this. I'd have some right to this feeling.' This insight is remarkable to me, writing as a middle-class young man who has never particularly experienced hardship or tragedy, except vicariously, but who would claim to have felt strong emotion in the course of my life. The guilt one feels at feeling sorrow when one has not experienced anything really qualifying as tragedy is a fascinating sensation, expertly picked out here by Gill as a symptom of self-absorption as well as of rational analysis of personal experience.

The heart of the play's silence, though, lies not in Michael but in the distance between the two men – *In the Blue* is, finally, a study of the limits of love. This is another recurrent theme in Gill's work: Michael echoes something Mrs Harte says about her children in *Small Change* when he tells Stewart, 'It's when you're not here I want you,' adding later, 'Yet there's another part of me that doesn't give a fuck.' Stewart, for his part, locates the heart of his problem in Michael:

Michael: What's the matter?
Stewart: You are.

In the series of imagined possible conversations between these two men, we are shown the extent to which the distance between two people is uncrossable.

★

Mean Tears was first performed in the Cottesloe auditorium of the National Theatre , London, on 22 July 1987, with the following cast:

Julian Bill Nighy
Stephen Karl Johnson
Paul Garry Cooper
Celia Hilary Dawson
Nell Emma Piper

Directed by Peter Gill
Designed by Alison Chitty
Lighting designed by Stephen Wentworth

★

"It's just I can't bear the thought of someone knowing more about you than me."

There is something purgatorial about the situation we are presented with in *In the Blue*, with Michael apparently bound into endlessly imagining and re-imagining his relationship with Stewart. This reading of modern life as purgatory is addressed more comprehensively in Gill's next play, *Mean Tears*, which is also set in contemporary London, and explores, among other things, a complex male relationship, and an underclass of people who are both educated and take heroin – people who seem to belong to the same society as Michael and Stewart. Engaging with the Catholic idea, developed from the Marian hymn 'Salve Regina', of life on this earth as exile ('Salve Regina' exhorts, 'show us the blessed fruit of your womb, after this our exile'), Julian observes in *Mean Tears*: 'I'm in purgatory', while Stewart says 'I'm like a dog scratching at the door,' offering another image of an individual trapped outside somewhere and trying to get in. Holman Hunt's famous painting of Christ standing with a lantern outside a door with no handle springs to mind, and most likely not unintentionally: Gill may fight shy of admitting to quoting Donne, but when it comes to Catholic doctrine his education by the Christian Brothers ensures references such as these are never made unknowingly.

Gill's portrait in *Mean Tears* is of a class drifting through life, convinced they are not quite part of it, sleepwalking through experience without taking real control of their days. Like *In the Blue*, the play's design framed it as a sketch, a provisional world appearing in outline before us: the setting is once again the indication of a room, this time that of the character Julian, which can be used to indicate other rooms when necessary. This sketched quality is further suggested by Gill's opening stage directions, which specify that breaks between scenes are not intended to slow the action on stage – a fluid slippage from sequence to sequence is suggested instead, one passage giving way like a wave to the next, a technique Gill had used in his work since *Over Gardens Out*, but which he now applied to a wider cast of characters and situations.

The play once again can be seen to develop in the context of previous work, standing as an example of Gill's handwriting being applied to a new subject and a new story. Stylistic continuities with previous plays extend to the enacting of an entire scene from *Over Gardens Out* – as Dennis ruins an evening for his parents in that play, forcing his father to stalk off and wait for his wife at the end of the road while she comforts their son, so Julian spoils a night at the pub for Stephen and Paul, with Paul playing the father and Stephen the mother, staying behind to comfort the difficult child. At the end of the play, a knife is drawn and not used, while earlier in the play we see other examples of characters

living vicariously through the performance of American stars –
Julian sings both Lou Reed and Bruce Springsteen during the
play, reaching after glamour that eludes him in his own life. The
world around him, for all its affectations, refuses to be as exciting
as it seems when Lou Reed describes it, while the peculiar and
poignant irony folded into an English character singing 'Born in
the USA', longing to care about something and not minding the
song is not for them, establishes the distance these characters
experience between themselves and the big world.

The world Gill presents is one of apparent pretension and
refinement: the play begins with Julian reading poetry to Stephen
then turning to him to say, 'isn't that great?' This prescient
Blairism (it is testament to Gill's ear that he caught the idiom of
Blair's generation and their particular bland of blokeish intellec-
tualism long before that idiolect was presented on the world stage
– the inquisitiveness and intelligence of its denizens sometimes
makes the theatre very good at breaking news) locates us among
the languid and lettered, people who are casual about their
reading, their ideas, their imaginations. The poem Julian chooses
to read locates this scene more precisely as something self-
consciously alternative, a would-be boho den freed from the
constraints of social norms. Julian opens the play by intoning, 'I
never was attached to that great sect', and as well as suggesting
to the listening audience a sense of detachment, of an alternative
world at bay from the big world, the 'great sect', goes on to read
a passage from Shelley about monogamy (or otherwise) and love.
Julian, it appears, is 'cool', a new pose for a Gill character, and a
studied and performed one at that, constructed out of poems,
adherence to very common 'alternative' ideas, and a frame of
reference familiar to most undergraduates – the second time he
reads poetry in the play, it is also a passage of Shelley. By this
time he is reading to someone else – a girl named Celia. Celia
listens to the reading and replies: 'I wrote an essay on
'Epipsychidion' when I was at university but I never read it.
There was a book out at the time. I cribbed from it.' So, we are
in the world of people who read about books, without actually
reading them, and the world of lettered young men who can only

actually quote one writer. Stephen later displays a nihilistic streak that is entirely in keeping with these cultural indicators: 'What do you mean, he's not worth it? Of course he's not worth it. Who is worth it?' This emotional distancing, the denial of sincere feeling, which is channelled into poetry instead, is at the centre of the pose these characters take.

These dislocated characters are far from unsympathetic, however. As well as self-indulgence and self-pity, we see them engaging in wit and conversation more compellingly and entertainingly than any previous cast of Gill's characters – this is the funniest, most erudite world he has shown us, a well read metropolitan crowd who entertain one another with their intelligence. As a result, *Mean Tears* is perhaps Gill's funniest play, laced with jokes in a way Gill had not previously attempted. These grow out of the interplay of the central characters, Julian and Stephen, whose sparring relationship ranges from the wrought and emotional to the good-natured and humorous:

> Stephen: He's about as lasting as Nelson Eddy David Bowie.
> Julian: Who's Nelson Eddy?

Julian stokes their friendship, as any close friend does with another, with the sharing of memories, the filling in of his own life for Stephen's entertainment, and amuses his friend with the memory of pranks he played at school:

> Julian: We used to find a telephone box, dial O and when the operator answered we used to say, 'Is that you, operator?' And she'd say, 'Yes', and we'd say, 'well, get off the line, there's a train coming'.

I adore this anecdote. It has the complexity of genuinely lived experience, and there is a poise and finesse, a studied element to the telling. The one time I tried to retell it myself to someone who didn't know the play, the story came out in the wrong order. It's very well written, and very hard to tell right.

Stephen, the play's deepest thinker and eventually its most

eloquent voice, proves himself well capable of matching Julian for
wit, as he shows in this sardonically deprecatory aside:

> Stephen: Julian, I am not the rock critic for Isis. I am not
> interested in the irony of the Velvet Underground as
> perceived by... Terry Jones. Cliff Richard has a
> perfectly good voice.

It takes real intelligence to phrase an argument in favour of
the music of Cliff Richard persuasively. Stephen displays a knack
for characterising, for summarising a personality with a bold
stroke (his reading of the Oxford undergraduate's approach to
music here is a glorious put-down that Julian chooses not to
engage with). He does so to most entertaining effect when
categorising women later in the play:

> Stephen: She's a hockey-field Venus. Half good-looking
> like you. Grew too tall to be a dancer, I shouldn't
> wonder. They live in Cambridge in one of those big
> houses on the Chesterton Road and her aunt was
> Wittgenstein's doctor's receptionist, or north Oxford
> and their mother was an actress, but gave it up to have
> nine brutally concerned children. Or she lopes along
> Chiswick Mall, the daughter of a judge. And gives you
> pebbles or driftwood for Christmas. Trouble. Take a
> very long spoon. I bet she went to the Band Aid
> concert.

The structure of these vignettes, each one developing from
plain location to a startling and comic cohering image –
'Wittgenstein's doctor's receptionist', 'nine brutally concerned
children', 'gives you pebbles or driftwood for Christmas', and the
final, curled-lip conclusion, 'I bet she went to the Band Aid
concert', another reminder of the studied non-commitment at
the heart of these characters – is both brilliant, and evidently the
technique of someone well practised in put-downs. Here is
someone who spends a lot of their time characterising others
wittily and dismissively – we are in the world of student banter,

and Stephen proves himself to have what every student prizes above all else - good chat. Gill displays both sides of this slacker culture – the lack of commitment to anything, but also the charming reasons they are able to get away with being the way they are.

The play is also a study of devotional love – amongst the non-commitments of the world Gill explores there is one character, Stephen, who is entirely fixated on another, Julian. This fixation is complicated by Julian's attitude during the play, as he abandons Stephen first for Celia and then for Nell, always returning to him but never committing as Stephen desires, never, apparently, equal in his love. Stephen finds this debilitating, and is powerless in the face of his emotion:

> Julian: Say.
> Stephen: No, I'm not saying. You work it out. Why should
>   I come out with a lot of recriminations? You're happy...
>   I'll – I'll just wait for the time when I can say – why did
>   I ever feel this about you? I look and watch and wait
>   for you like a kid outside a pub sitting on the kerb or a
>   step.

Like all strong emotion, Stephen's feelings for Julian are essentially inexpressible. He cannot put into words the numinous significance he finds in Julian, though he tries:

> Stephen: You've got some light. Some glow. I find myself
>   crying and you know – I don't even know what it is I'm
>   feeling. I don't know if I'm unhappy or not. I don't
>   even fucking like you. I've located a part of myself in
>   you. And I dread the feeling in the future of my sense
>   of worthlessness now at having been so shallow all the
>   time.

His conviction that he is debasing himself, and his inability to do anything about it, are moving testament to the emotional sea he is adrift in. His feelings for Julian govern his whole life, shaping his attitudes to the world and the world's seeming actions towards him. Everything he does happens in the context of Julian:

> Stephen: I hear something on the radio and I laugh because it's going to be something I like and I think, got you, you bastard. Then I feel the pain of wanting to share it with you – pain that you wouldn't really want to... and then I feel I can't sustain the hate – the feeling current in me is too weak and the tears start and then, to cap it all, before our next programme they play Schubert's 'Seligheit'.

The remorseless complicity of the radio controller indicates Stephen's broader attitude towards the world around him, which he sees as hostile and life-sapping, an attitude he expresses with extraordinary eloquence to Stephen. Anyone who has lived in London has felt like this from time to time, but it has rarely been better phrased:

> Stephen: I have to have some defence.
> Julian: Against what?
> Stephen: That place.
> Julian: Where? Work? Against what?
> Stephen: The mendacity. The envy. The fear. The lack of principle. The mismanagement, the lack of vision, the self-interest. One's self-interest. The atmosphere of witch-hunt, the wish to make things worse. The mishandling, the pusillanimity. The unkindness. The lack of any care, the lack of guts to even stab Caesar when he's dead. 'Speak hands for me'. The trivial nature, the residue of complacency and dissatisfaction and graft. The exhausted ideals, the lack of perspective, the dead wood, the mediocrity, the vacillation, the meanness of spirit, the gutless, not even opportunism. The terminal air.

This is great poetry: a T.S. Eliot vision of modern London that Gill has gestured towards before, in Gerard's speeches in

Small Change, but now expresses more directly. In its range of reference, and the sweep of its dismissal of urban impulses, it is chilling, and stands out in the play as a moment of keen-eyed clear thinking among the romances, intrigues and fighting. Elsewhere Stephen seems to wheedle, to depend, telling Julian that 'if I was in jail you'd forget to come or come late.' But we are reminded by his intelligence, and by these occasional outbursts, who it is who has been made so dependent on another who does not truly care for him and how sad his predicament is. He is trapped, diverted from whatever course it seems he should be taking. The tragedy of the play is that this brings him no new happiness. He and Julian both experience a distance between them that is difficult to cross:

> Julian: I don't exist for you, Stephen, really. You'd like to
> blow me out.
> Stephen: Do you know, we don't know who the other is.

Though Stephen seems deadly accurate when he says of Julian, 'It's the pure filament of self-obsession,' Gill shows us the obsessions of these characters are the result of their insecurities (all arrogance or self-absorption seems to me to be the product of insecurity at its heart), as the apparently confident Julian repeatedly asks his friends, 'Is this shirt OK?', and later confides to Stephen that 'I feel I'm locked in a tennis court and people keep serving balls to me and I have to play and I can't compete.' Stephen relates their situation back to the earlier generation of Romantics when he asks, 'what's the opposite of negative capability? Positive incapacity.' This is what afflicts Gill's new romantics: talent, and the inability or disinclination to do anything with it. Stephen, speaking to Paul, evokes a sense of people experiencing life at arm's length, watching it across a distance rather than living it themselves:

> Stephen: There was this play and a man on a park bench
> and he said, 'I feel I haven't been part of life.'
> Something like that. Have you been part of life?
> Paul: I don't know what that means.

> Stephen: It goes through one, I suppose, in its own way. If we will let life live us instead of being afraid of or thinking other lives should be our lives. It's our own life we must live.

What they have instead of any experience of belonging to anything is a sense of displacement, as Julian communicates to Nell:

> Julian: I'm restless.
> Nell: No.
> Julian: Not with you. I don't know what I'm doing. Work. Everything. I'm a sort of displaced person. I feel like some sort of refugee here.

Nell responds to this by speaking of Border Country:

> Nell: There is something utterly strange and compelling and beautiful about Border Country, I think... I went to Wales once and we got to somewhere out of Shakespeare... Mortimer's Cross. And I got this feeling, scary. Beautiful. I expected Red Indians. But our Borders...

Nell is, in fact, talking of her home in Scotland, but she speaks of her own situation as well. These characters inhabit borders, between the respectable and disreputable, between generations and classes and aspirations. Stephen comments that 'young people are like unborn babies', and it is this strange, undecided state Nell also seems to allude to, a borderland of potential and unrealised possibilities. Once again, we see in Nell a reaching after the weight and glamour of the big world – her getting to 'somewhere out of Shakespeare' is like enacting Brando or Dean, or singing Elvis – a way of trying to connect with the world around and interact with someone whose life, in her eyes, had weight.

These people languish in their situation, trapped in drifting lives that do not quite satisfy them. Julian evokes one of Gill's central continuing themes when he says, 'I wish I could change'. Stephen responds to his attitude with exasperation: 'For fuck's sake, you're young, young. Be young.' Gill is also showing us a world of isolated people – Stephen comments on 'the loneliness of all those people, lonely. They'd be less unhappy if they knew they were just lonely.' This self-knowledge should, he claims, comfort him – but he, more than perhaps anyone else in the play, proves incapable of being young, of living in the present.

While Stephen lives his life in imagination, wanting Julian and caring only for him, Julian is trapped in the past, a victim of his childhood, suffering in the shadow of his father: 'my father insured me. I fucking hate him,' and haunted by memories of a childhood spent at a distance from the world – he says of boarding school, 'the worst time was having to go to bed at seven in the summer evenings with the light through the curtains. That was the worst time.' He is not alone in the play in being in retreat and recovery from his childhood, and recognises the same impulse in others, acutely diagnosing the unspoken in Nell:

> Nell: I love going home. In spite of... Mainly for the place.
>   The village. The town. Our house and when we're all
>   together, I suppose.
> Julian: In spite of what? What does your father do?

Stephen, as well, locates at one point in the play the source of his present unhappiness in his childhood: 'I think I was a very loving child and never grew out of it.' This reading, of delayed adulthood as the centre of these uncertain lives, seems to be at the heart of their own ideas of themselves.

However, as with all of Gill's work, and indeed with any good play, it is in the subtext rather than the text that the real sources of these people's insecurities are located. We have seen before, in *The Sleepers Den* most effectively, what a very inadequate last resort blaming one's parents for one's failures is – a coalescence of inadequacies around the person nearest at hand, rather than a real diagnosis. *Mean Tears*, therefore, while locating some of the unhappinesses of its characters in the generation before them, also studies the turbulence under the surfaces of the different protagonists – it is, first of all, a study of people dealing with subterranean feeling, not of feelings which can be brought constructively into the light and resolved. This, it seems to me, is the useful function of fiction – the examination of and engagement with those aspects of our life which are irresolvable, which cannot be argued or debated or psychoanalysed away but are part of us, and carried with us always. Jung said it was the purpose of his psychoanalysis to ensure that great men retained their neuroses; I believe he may have been overstating his abilities. Much of our psychic baggage, the psychic fat and rind Gill writes of in *Small Change*, seems permanent to me. This does not, however, mean it does not require analysis and confrontation; quite the contrary. A chronic condition such as being alive must receive constant attention, and that is something art does well, allowing us to circle and test the problem of ourselves.

Julian and Stephen gesture towards their own regard for this subtext to the surface of their dialogues when they discuss opera:

> Julian: What's Fidelio about?
> Stephen: Well, there's...
> Julian: No, no, no. What's it about?
> Stephen: It's about freedom and constancy.

Nell guesses at hidden influences in her own relationship with Julian, who confesses when she challenges him that the play's central relationship, his own with Stephen, has a tidal pull on his relationship with Nell:

> Nell: Stephen's in this, isn't he? Isn't he?
> Julian: No. Well, people are in everything, aren't they?

This concession, that the past and the absent are always present, informing and shaping events which have no seeming relation to them, reveals the hidden momentum of the play, which is a struggling to live under the weight of memory and emotion. These emotions, Stephen suggests, cannot be accessed directly:

> Stephen: One has to say other things when one wants not
> to speak at all but to say please or help or love or please
> or cry. Over and over and over.

The characters speak in screen exchanges, to borrow Freud's term, constructing interactions out of the mundane that present the sincere and painful emotions at the heart of them from coming to the surface. It is in this sleep, not a sleep of sloth or carelessness, that they live their lives, and the realisation of this demands sympathy for these feckless, drifting people. At the end of the play, Stephen retaliates to Julian's erudite readings of poetry by reciting 'Little Boy Blue', closing the play with an image of Julian, but also of the whole world we have been exposed to, as distant from their real lives, shielded from real emotion, sleeping away their youth:

> Stephen: Will I wake him? No not I. For if I do he is sure
> to cry. Isn't that great?

The final, despairing repetition of Julian's own literary commentary – 'Isn't that great'? – makes a mockery of the pretensions of the characters through the play, stripping away manner and erudition to access, for once, though still at arm's length and through poetry, but at least this time through something simple that seeks to take the characters closer to the centre of themselves by drawing them back into memories of childhood, a sincere emotion.

What these characters long to do is matter. Julian expresses this first, speaking to Celia:

> Julian: I'd like to see your face change because of me. I
> saw it light up because of me. At the door. I just want
> to have that effect on you again. That's all. I just want
> to fuck you to see you change.

This statement is set in a wider context at the close of the play by Stephen, who passes comment on the entire world, the entire play, judging the poses they adopt:

> Stephen: What Lady Caroline Lamb said about Byron has lent glamour to all the cheap irresponsibilities of people like you and Nell ever since, without acknowledging that Byron actually produced something at least as substantial as all the misery he must have caused.

The desire Julian has earlier expressed, the source of insecurity elsewhere, the need to matter to someone, is placed by Stephen in a larger final context, as their affectations are made to look tawdry and false in the face of their lack of achievement, their inability to mean anything positive to anyone.

This is a major play about the psychological revolution engendered by Thatcherism. The director Lucy Maycock, speaking about divorce rates at the end of the last century, observed when we met and spoke about Gill that it was the 80s which, ironically, lengthened the odds on a marriage lasting the distance (an interesting legacy for Thatcher, the undermining of one aspect of her ostensible personal philosophy by the logical consequence of the propagation of other aspects of the same muddled value system, and a reminder that conservatism and capitalism are relatively difficult creeds to reconcile. I have never quite understood how Thatcherite attitudes towards the primacy of the family and the primacy of the individual were philosophically compatible). The drive toward self-realisation, which was the product of the Thatcherite 'on-yer-bike' culture, was naturally going to extend into the personal world and lead to a lot of people deciding that in order to fully realise their lives they would need to leave their not ideally happy marriages. This is not necessarily a bad thing: the explosion of divorce rates after Thatcher in part tells us how many people in the history of our culture before that time were probably putting up with things they might rather not have tolerated, had the tenor of the times been otherwise. However, promoting individualism and thereby, at a basic theoretical level, logically undermining old-fashioned ideas of the dignity of labour, collective work or work unlikely to lead to acclaim and advancement, as well as the primacy of the family unit (why settle for anything when you could go for more?) led to life being lived between two polarities. On the one hand there was the rejection of ambition and growth as the basic motivating forces in a life in favour of a rootedness which manifested itself during the period variously in defences of place, trades, histories and cultures, and which Thatcherism sought an illogical foothold in when it attempted to promote the family at the same time as promoting the individual. On the other was the wholehearted embrace of individualism and self-realisation as a governing creed, which manifested itself as the pursuit of gain at the expense of social solidarity or anything W.H. Davies might have called a life worth examining. The by-product of this second extreme is, of course, massive self-absorption. Gill's play is a study of this toxic by-product of the culture of the time – the way an obsession with the value of one's self and an unmooring from all previous social structures could in fact do quite the opposite of what capitalism sets out to achieve: rather than allowing growth, it can strangle people into narcissism and self-involve-ment. As a study of the fate of a generation – a generation who would go on to dismantle the political left in this country and allow capitalism to come very close to eating itself – *Mean Tears* has proved a prescient road map towards the trouble our current leaders have got themselves into.

6. PANORAMAS
THE NATIONAL THEATRE AND THE NATIONAL
THEATRE STUDIO, *CARDIFF EAST* AND *CERTAIN*
YOUNG MEN

The culmination of all Gill's directorial work at the Royal Court, Riverside Studios and around Europe and America came in 1980, when he was appointed an Associate Director of the National Theatre. Appointments such as this have a marvellous double function for those who benefit from them, as was the case with Gill. His new role confirmed and rewarded the quality of what he had achieved already, reaffirming his reputation as one of the leading directors of his generation. It also afforded him the resources and the platform to capitalise on the talent and imagination he had previously developed and demonstrated and establish his distinctive vision of the theatre in the public consciousness, providing him as it did with resources that allowed him to work with a renewed intensity on a sustained run of major productions. Between 1981 and 1997 directed a succession of productions that should be considered as the main body of his work, the cornerstone of his achievement in the theatre. He directed an eclectic repertoire of major plays, including *A Month in the Country, Much Ado About Nothing, Danton's Death, Major Barbara, Antigone, Venice Preserv'd* and *Juno and the Paycock,* and the writers he worked with during this period of sustained success included Isaiah Berlin, John Fowles, Howard Brenton, Christopher Hampton, Sam Shepard and Nicholas Wright. If this were a biographical study of Gill, this mature phase of his work as an artist would take up a great number of words and pages – it was here that the lessons he had learned and the reputation he had gained at the Royal Court, at Riverside Studios and while directing around the world was supplied with the sustained resources needed for Gill to fully realise his talents as a director, where his distinctive aesthetic was given a major public platform. However, such detail must be supplied by another book. As I have said before, this is a study of an aesthetic, not a career. Gill's work during this period expounded and developed this aesthetic, of course, but the most interesting innovations and developments Gill made during the period lay not on the stage, nor even in the rehearsal room – but in the old National Theatre Paintframe by the Old Vic Theatre on The Cut, which, in 1984, had its use converted and became the National Theatre Studio.

Peter Hall established the National Theatre Studio for political as well as practical reasons – creating a space for work to be done without the pressure of production would lead to the development of artists who could go on to work on the National's stages, but the Studio was also an emphatic statement about the values of the theatre as an organisation with a serious commitment to theatre as art, to the development of new work, to being at the forefront of innovation. Gill's appointment as the Studio's Director, a natural development of the work he had done at Riverside Studios, gave him an extraordinary opportunity to develop the aesthetic of his work through workshops and sustained engagement with the craft of the theatre. This process informed and underpinned his work on the National's stages. Some of his productions developed directly from work done at the Studio – *In The Blue* began as part of a workshop without a script, and was presented as part of a festival of new plays from the Studio, and plays such as Daniel Mornin's *The Murderers* were also developed directly as a result of Studio work. But the Studio at that time was not primarily intended to develop work directly for the National's stages. Instead, it was a place where young directors could have an opportunity to work on plays; where the plays of new writers could receive readings; where resources were made available to talent with the intention of sparking new creativity. Gill undertook workshops of his own as part of this wider programme of creative ferment, and was able to follow a wide-ranging creative brief. The most fondly remem-

bered workshop of his time there, by himself and many of his
collaborators at the Studio, was an afternoon when Gill invited
Gwen Ffrangcon-Davies, who was then in her nineties but had
played Juliet opposite John Gielgud in 1924, to come to the
Studio and read the part. Directors present at this event recall it
as revelatory – an elderly woman drawing on the technique of a
century earlier to deliver verse with a clarity and beauty that they
had not heard in the part before. Another project led to Gill's
production of his own adaptation of *As I Lay Dying*, which grew
out of a workshop. The play was built around tableaux – actors
had to adopt exaggerated poses of grief and then expand them
into new poses as the play developed, so that the production
resembled a series of animated Gericault paintings.

The resources of the National Theatre Studio allowed Gill to
fully develop and articulate his practical philosophy of theatre,
and to have a major influence on a generation of artists who
worked with him there early in their careers. His own writing
expanded in scale – not just in terms of cast size, but also in terms
of formal complexity and the subject matter it addressed –
dramatically during the period, and his approach to theatre was
fully formulated and worked out by a sustained engagement with
a regular company of collaborators of a shared temperament.
Gill's project, as recalled by contemporaries at the Studio, was to
make theatre that was about the body in space; to make a theatre
where the right actors were cast in the right parts, which
challenged the idea that an Oxford graduate with a knack for
accents was suitable for everything; for a theatre whose moral
project, as a broadly social realist school, was to develop work
that showed the world as it was and demanded people look at it.
However, the most significant product of all this activity in my
judgement was the dramatic expansion of Gill's mind and his
creative palette – a development clearly visible in the two most
complex and intricate theatrical structures he has built to date,
one of which was produced at the National and the other
immediately after his period as an Associate there – his
panoramic, dance-like explorations of two very different social
worlds, *Cardiff East* and *Certain Young Men*.

Cardiff East was first performed in the Cottesloe auditorium of the National Theatre, London, on 6 February 1997 with the following cast:

Neil – Daniel Evans
Stella – June Watson
Tommy – Matthew Rhys
Annie – Gwenllian Davies
Darkie – Andrew Howard
Anne-Marie – Lowri Palfrey/Stacey Nelson
Ryan – Alex Parker/Richard Pudney
Michael – Kenneth Cranham
Shirley – Melanie Hill
Billy – Mark Lewis Jones
Marge – Susan Brown
Dolly – Elizabeth Estensen
Vera – Di Botcher
Carol – Lisa Palfrey
Len – Karl Johnson
Charlie – Windsor Davies
Bingo Caller's Voice – Anthony O'Donnell

Directed by Peter Gill
Designed by Alison Chitty
Lighting by Andy Phillips
Music by Terry Davies

★

Mean Tears had been a significant expansion of the canvas and scope of Gill's work – a development that was partly the result of access to greater resources made available by the support of the National Theatre, but which had also seen Gill expand his fictional world, addressing new subjects, attempting new breadth as he sought to capture the character of a generation and a social strata, growing beyond the memorial canvases of his Royal Court plays to present society more confrontationally and completely to

itself. This expansion of subject matter, and an expansion in the
scale of the work he was writing in terms of company size and
narrative breadth, now led to the writing of two extraordinary
plays – *Cardiff East* and *Certain Young Men*. These, again, were
portraits of a world. They are among Gill's most compelling
statements, still completely connected to the intensity of humanist feeling which had animated his early work, but now realised
on a larger scale, as social plays posing new and larger questions.

Cardiff East clearly illustrates the technical and imaginative
development made possible by Gill's move to the National
Theatre's stages, as, with access to a larger public forum, Gill
revisits the Cardiff of his early plays, but this time with a
panoramic eye, collecting experience into a larger statement. All
the isolation, frustration, desperation and hunger of *The Sleepers
Den* and *Over Gardens Out* is present in the play, and as with
Small Change the voices are captured out of love, a love of what
is lost and what can be remembered back into being – but Gill
weaves together a greater number of voices and stories, showing
more, and finds himself able to portray something new about the
city he came from. In *Cardiff East* a society is shown that
surmounts the individual stories of Gill's individual characters, a
group of people linked by shared experience who Gill presents as
defiantly alive, unshiftably as real and compelling as the world
they feel distant from.

Once more, the aesthetic of the play is stark, and draws all
focus to the bodies on stage: most of the characters in *Cardiff
East* never leave the sparsely furnished playing area, but remain
still and visible while they are not active. The characters
themselves are the dressing of the play, an appropriate picture, as
they, not the part of Cardiff they live in, are of course the subject.
The play tells the story of a day among a community of people
living in close proximity to each other, beginning and ending
with the characters going to bed on two consecutive nights – the
action between these two sequences passes the day. What we are
shown in this period is a disparate collection of characters, each
perhaps trapped within their own small lives and social circles,
but connected by shared experience to a larger community which

the play seeks to capture. . There is more than a touch of *Ulysses* about Gill's chosen dramatic structure, as the ordinary acts of ordinary people are given all the attention of heroics, given the same space and time and attention as Odysseus, or Leopold Bloom.

The play begins with a stage strewn with characters waiting, already asleep, or unable to sleep and about to take a pill. It is a series of images of isolation that first confronts us, each character seeming locked in the cell of themselves and looking alone. Neil, already in bed, is joined by his friend Tommy, who has just come from his girlfriend's house and talks his way into bed and then, eventually, into sexual closeness with Neil, a seduction that is obviously familiar to both of them, an old routine Neil tries to resist but doesn't really want to. The closeness of these two boys getting in bed together strains against the distance Neil wants to put between them, and he is powerless to resist it. Tommy, enacting a ritual he wants and betrays no guilt for, is playful, almost light in his behaviour, responding to Neil's entreaty to 'keep your hands to yourself' with a cheeky 'I might' as he slips between the sheets.

Meanwhile, Annie, elsewhere on stage and in Cardiff, is alone and unable to face the night undrugged, though she wishes she could: 'If I could sleep without anything, that would be a good thing, it would be... I should say my prayers, that's what I should do.' A generation before her, prayers were what Mrs Shannon resorted to as well, along with Guinness. Now Annie has recourse to sleeping pills, and they, not faith, have become her coping mechanism of choice, allowing her to bear the weight her life seems to carry in the evenings. The play is patterned with drug use – Tommy owes Darkie money for a different kind of coping mechanism, a familiar, pathetic method of escape from the everyday:

> Tommy: And I owes Darkie money.
> Neil: What for?
> Tommy: He got some stuff down the docks.
> Neil: What stuff? You're soft, you are. That's a mug's
>   game, that is. You want to quit that, you do. You don't

> want to do that, do you hear me, Tommy? Do you?
> You can't stuff your mother's wages up your nose.

Darkie himself doses up for the evening, for a third and different reason:

> Darkie takes a pill.
> Stella: What are you taking that for? What's that?
> Darkie: I got a headache.

This is a world of medicated struggle, in which people get by rather than live. There is need of drugs because actual happiness is in short supply, as Stella says to her son when he comes home on the same evening:

> Stella: I don't think they're very cheerful. Lisa's off work.
> Darkie: Oh aye.
> Stella: I don't think they're very happy.
> Darkie: I don't suppose they are.

The 'they' in this exchange seem to be the second family of Darkie's father, Stella's ex-husband – a second chance at life that went neither better nor worse than the first one, being subject to the same influences and limits. Stella sees the same patterns repeating in her son as well, though he denies them:

> Stella: Picking up crumbs like your father.
> Darkie: I'm not like my father.

Darkie's denial rings hollow and sad, as Stella goes on to worry him about girls, and the life he lives begins to sound like the life everyone might be living nearby him. Stella herself experiences repetition of old patterns in her own feelings:

> Stella: This is why your father went.
> Darkie: Why? He went because of that other piece.
> Stella: I couldn't cope.
> Darkie: You mean he couldn't cope.

Stella: Well, I couldn't.
Darkie: He couldn't cope.

Her fear, her lack of self-confidence, and Darkie's attempt at reassurance, as weak as the attempt to deny he is like his father, sounds like a drowning woman, her head going under for the second time of three. The patterns are there, and they can do no more than fight to be free of them. Across the stage, Neil experiences the same problem, pulled back by a similar tide into familiar experience, and gives in to it:

Neil: Leave me alone, you queer bent bastard.
Tommy: You like it.
Neil: I don't.
Tommy: Afterwards you don't, in a minute you will. Give
    me your hand.
He takes Neil's hand and puts it under the bedclothes.
Tommy: That's better.
Neil: Stop it, Tommy.
Tommy: Ssh, ssh, turn into me.
Neil: Don't, Tommy.
Tommy: Come on.
Neil: Don't.
Tommy: Come on, Neil.
Neil turns into Tony.
Tommy: Yeah, that's right.
Neil: Do it quiet.

These different goings to bed display a diffracted society, but the effect is curious, because they undoubtedly portray a coherent community as well: a rag-bag of different people brought together in the act of doing the same thing at about the same time, whose life's rhythms seem to connect them, though by little more than accident. What we see is the breaking of a wave of time around an object, throwing the object into sharp relief. As the scene proceeds, a domestic argument erupts onstage, overheard by the other characters, connecting them in what they listen to as Shirley accuses Billy of drinking his redundancy money. Shirley, like Stella, like Mrs Harte and Mrs Driscoll, seems to be struggling to cope: 'he just pushes me. He gets me in this state so I will say anything. He starts me. He makes me feel bad.' Elsewhere on stage, at once isolated from all around her and connected by sharing the same anxieties, the same feelings, Annie is the clearest image of unease in this Breughel-like, intercutting introduction, closing the scene with the sad admission that 'I can't sleep.'

The play's second scene also depicts collective experience. It is morning, and the characters are worrying about money. We are shown a world whose horizons are tragically limited – Annie becoming a centre of attention for a tiny win on the Lottery sets a scale of achievement and ambition which sustains through the exchanges that make up the scene:

> Vera: I heard you won ten pounds on the lottery.
> Annie: I did, I won ten pounds.

The poignancy of her pride at this is matched by the sweep of Vera's description of her own gambling venture of choice, when she says of Castle Bingo:

> It's like Las Vegas over there. You should see the Ladies –
>   gold taps and soap dishes. They went first week, the
>   soap dishes.

These are, of course, different escapes, different entertainments used like drugs to illuminate a life. Vera shows herself to be wryly aware that the glamour of Castle Bingo is only a surface when she talks about the soap dishes getting stolen within a week of the place opening – she knows the world she is in, and finds comedy in the imposition of a bingo hall with gold taps. She doesn't fall for it – rather, she allows herself to believe in it, as theatre, as an entertainment, and talks it up as a way of buying into the glamour she knows it fails to bring into her life. The patina of sadly tacky attractions extends from the Lottery and the bingo hall to another familiar touchstone, Elvis worship:

> Vera: He still going to Gracelands, next door? He tried to
> sell the house to go to Gracelands.
> Marge: He never.
> Vera: He tried to sell the house to go to Gracelands. For
> the funeral, mind you. He wanted to sell the house. He
> wanted to sell the house.

Again, Vera and Marge are aware of how ridiculous this story is, how mad that someone should try and sell their house to get to Elvis's funeral – but though they know it's silly, still they talk about it, still it goes on around them. It is a frame of cultural reference they wryly suffer, an ironic understanding and recognition of all that is drab about their lives:

> Marge: Well, at least it's not Tina Turner, they had Tina
> Turner the last time I went to the crematorium.

However, once again, though they know these things are terrible really, they tolerate them, and as their conversation proceeds we are reminded that they must live within the paleness of their lives as well as comment on them. When Vera comments that 'still, he got a pool table in there. He haven't done so bad', she hints at a criteria for judging success that seems to explain why, as well as bemoaning the use of 'Simply The Best' as a song at a funeral, this community might also tolerate it. When a pool table is a marker of success, when aspiration and ambition and achievement are hobbled to that extent, it becomes clear why one might make a deal out of winning ten pounds on the lottery. Vera extends this suspicion when she describes her last holiday:

> Vera: We went on holiday to Tenerife. She booked the
> holiday, I took my niece, we always go. The apartment,
> it was... well, you should have see it. I wouldn't have
> cleaned my floors with the towels in the bathroom. A
> very nice boy, the tour operator. Lovely. Tim. Well, the
> other people were as shocked as us, and we got put in
> the nice hotel. We had a lovely time, it's volcanic, the
> one beach. Anyway, she wrote a letter of complaint for

me and I got a letter back this morning, with a cheque
for fifty pounds. Always complain, see. It's right.

Knowing this is the escape Vera makes when she wants to get
out of her daily life shows us, again, the limits of her horizons.

I'm not entirely comfortable with what I have just written. I
feel like Synge with his ear to the wall. My grandparents owned
a pool table. It was not their proudest possession, but it had a
room of its own, the billiards room, which, seeing as they built the
house they lived in, was clearly important to them. It was the best
thing about their house to my mind. I thought it the height of
cool that when I went to see my grandparents I could play pool.
So if I've thought pool tables brilliant in my own life, why do I
find them sad when I read them in a play? Perhaps I am experiencing the familiar discomfort of seeing aspects of one's own life
on stage, the reticence that is always part of the response to
having attention paid to you, the feeling, so difficult to shake, that
if something's happened to you it can't possibly be worth anyone
else looking at. My response to the pool table in *Cardiff East* is
also, I think, the result of a conviction that nothing in a play
means only its surface meaning. Everything in a play simultaneously means several things as it happens, many of them often
contradictory. That is inherent in the richness of language and of
metaphor, which is at the heart of the theatre. A play is a
metaphor that has been cornered in the dark of a theatre, which
is never glimpsed whole but lit up by scene after scene like the
beams of different torches, until by the end of the evening we
have seen the whole of the monster in the dark, its different parts
glimpsed for us to piece together for ourselves. So a pool table is
never just a pool table in a play – it is also a torch being shone to
illuminate something else.

I am aware these comments I am making on a portrayal of life
in a working class area are tending towards the slightly obtuse.
The snobbishness of calling the Lottery small, of looking at a
reading of life and reducing it to a class-based criticism, does not
escape me. But I find it difficult not to read *Cardiff East* through
a politicising filter. Just as the motivating action of D.H.

Lawrence's plays seems to me to be that vital line in *A Collier's Friday Night*, 'as many things happen for you as happen for me', so the action of this play is surely, in part, to say 'look at this. These people are living, they are as alive as you'. So how can we avoid wondering why we have been asked to look, and making observations about the lives we see in a search for an explanation? If the suspicion arises that we have been cast as Synge, that Gill has got us eavesdropping on these people, that must be interrogated. When this play was first produced at the National Theatre, the eavesdropping effect must have been even more marked than it is on the page, after all: the juxtaposition of the National's habitual audience with the world of *Cardiff East* is a stark contrast.

This is a conversation I have had with Max Stafford-Clark, whose programming of Andrea Dunbar's *The Arbor* at the Royal Court raised similar questions for me. What was the action of that play, about a girl growing up on an estate in Bradford, when Dunbar was writing it on a Bradford estate at the age of fifteen? Was that the same action the play possessed when it opened to a suited and booted crowd in Sloane Square? I think of a comment Dunbar made in rehearsals – 'it weren't so funny when it was happening' – and that translation of life into line, which Gill also performs here, seems to me to be motivated in part out of the desire to present life in a certain place and ask an audience to use the context for that life they bring to the theatre to draw certain inferences from the juxtaposition of those two worlds. That is where the political argument of the play is hidden, waiting for us to find it and fill it in.

Having concealed the play's political argument, Gill is liberated to devote his attention to the people in the play, to write on a humanist scale that refuses to reduce his characters to the arguments I risk making them when I try to write about the blanks and the inference in the text. This sequence of the play features prime examples of what Gill does perhaps more extraordinarily than any other writer – the burial of emotion in the small acts of daily life, through which we are allowed to glimpse the motivating emotions of characters and lives. Here is Marge worrying about washing: 'To think I used to get pleasure out of washing his shirts. I didn't have a washing machine for... oo... I used Mam's. No, he's good. They're all good. They'll all put them in the machine. Tony all his decent clothes, he won't let me touch them. When I was washing his shirts when we were first married I could feel his mother watching me.' This is great writing about love. How she felt about her husband after they were married escapes through the act of ironing shirts; how proud she was of her boys escapes through memories of them putting their clothes in the wash; her feelings for her mother in law escape through the attention she paid to collars and cuffs. This is where life is lived, in detail. Craig Raine writes in his poem 'A la recherché du temps perdu':

> The writer makes things real.
> His task: 'to make you hear, to make you feel –
>
> It is, before all, to make you see.
> To make you see. Before all. I agree.
>
> 'That – and no more, and it is everything.'
> Details that make you cringe
>
> Will make the reader see,
> See the self you showed to me.

This is a lesson Gill understands and deploys brilliantly. We see Annie exploring the negotiations that sustain relationships through a memory of ironing and corned beef: 'Harry always thought I washed his shirts by hand till the day he died because I always put them on a hanger. He never knew. But then he liked corned beef from the shop, he didn't like it from a tin.' The subtlety with which Gill expresses the indulgences and sleights of hand Annie lavished on her husband, and the love she had for him, makes for a compelling and luminous picture.

Nor is this just technical skill. Gill's ability to approach emotion sideways is important because he is writing here about the way we all experience emotion, the way we all experience life.

Auden wrote in 'As I Walked Out One Evening', 'In headaches and in worry/ Vaguely life slips away.' It is among these small details life is lived, the big projects lost among to-do lists, appointments, the ordinary and everyday. What Gill shows us, though, is that it is through close attention to those headaches, to that worry, that life can also be reclaimed – that an excavation of those smaller things can give us access to the larger feelings hiding behind them. This is the only way we could have glimpsed the love Annie had for her husband. This is the way it was expressed.

The last escape the scene details lies in faith – or rather, in the trappings of it. Throughout the scene, the characters are seen singing songs they heard on *Songs of Praise* and trying to remember Schubert's 'Ave Maria'. We can see this is the background sound of their lives rather than an active preoccupation – no one can remember how the tune goes, and Michael observes jokingly that 'It's one of the conundrums of Christianity, that no one can remember 'Ave Maria'.' However, at the close of the scene we are treated to it once, when Annie sings the piece once through. This is a striking echo of the decade of the rosary at the heart of *The Sleepers Den* – a resort to ritual as an entertainment, which also represents an escape from and a glamorisation of daily life, that is still somehow sad for being not a song they know or care about, but something they heard on the TV.

The play's next scene shows us the source of these different manifestations of escape – diagnosing the need felt in the anxiety and insecurity of Shirley, who recalls Mrs Driscoll when she says: 'Just don't leave. I'm in a panic you're going to leave. I'll dissolve. I will. I'm dissolving. I'll dissolve, dissolve, I'd be gone. Oh. I'd be glad to be gone. Oh, oh. Don't go, I'm asking you.' Shirley's worries are not just a need for others, but a fundamental uncertainty about herself: 'Why am I a mother, not a woman? Why are men? It makes me feel bad. Why won't someone break through, why won't someone tell me what to do?' Fear is proposed as a basic state of being:

> Marge: You're so frightened when you're young.
> Dolly: I'm frightened now.

What is shown to us is the extent to which these characters live with compromise as a basic part of their day. Shirley says of her husband, 'He'd say make the best of it, of everything... use everything. Find a new use for old things, live as in a siege, teach yourself to be master of a siege situation.' The ordinary day we are watching here is described as a siege, characterised by desperation and shortage and ingenuity. The lives being lived onstage are also characterised by loss and the constant falling away of old ideals, as these people are left stranded in old ways and habits as the tide of the world seems to go out on them:

> Marge: I don't know who comes home to dinner now.
> Vera: No one I know.
> Dolly: My mother-in-law still cooks dinner.

Values are maintained among this generation that seem to have been forgotten or decreed unimportant elsewhere. This is, of course, hardly an unusual reading of life. It is a ubiquitous experience that the world moves on around individuals, and the characters recognise it in everything around them:

> Dolly: What was all here before there was houses here?
> Annie: Oh, I lived in town. This was all the wilds for me...
> Michael: This was all moorland here. This was all
> moorland caught between two rivers, the Taff and the
> Rumney river. The old sea wall and the gut that run
> alongside it must have been built to protect animals. It
> was so flat and wide, all at sea level. It was so flat and
> wide, all at sea level. There were all farms out here at
> one time, not all farms because of the tides.

Gill did not direct a play in his home town until 2012. Julia Wyndham, his assistant on the production of *A Provincial Life*, told me that every cab journey with him during rehearsals was a lecture tour of a vanished Cardiff, as Gill, staring out the window, would tell her and the driver how each street had looked in the years of his childhood. I suggested to Peter there might be a story in that, in documenting a vanished world, thinking of Joyce's aspiration for Ulysses that, should Dublin ever burn down, it would be possible to rebuild the city with nothing but his novel for reference, and of Ciaran Carson's *The Star Factory*, a journey through memories of a city. Gill replied 'yes, but that happens everywhere, doesn't it.' It was not until after this time that I began working seriously on this book, at which point I realised the story I had suggested was already present in his plays, woven through everything he had ever written about Cardiff – but I am glad I hadn't done my homework, because Peter's answer to my proposal led me to believe that what he sought to write here, as well as a portrait of a group of people, was a universal experience, a way of looking at everything by looking at one place and one time. This is always the best way of accessing ideas, of course – if we can engage constructively in detail as a way of exploring larger questions, we're more likely to be able to actually say something, to use proper nouns instead of generalities. That is, in fact, the project I am engaged with in this book – I have been writing about a particular approach to life, a particular way of seeing, which I believe I can best access by reading the plays of Peter Gill.

As well as decrying the loss of shared communal time as she knew it, Dolly also criticises new manifestations of community spirit and family solidarity, addressing funerals: 'I don't like too many flowers. There's too many flowers, it's got too much. I don't believe in it.' Dolly and Marge, commenting on current fashions at a slight remove, are wry and knowing in their skewering of trends, as we see when Dolly asks about the naming of a baby:

> Dolly: What's she call it?
> Marge: Some daft name I expect, Amy Pearl, Heidi Louise. Ellie Lou. Saffron. [*Marge is making Dolly laugh.*] Madison. Dakota. Ebbw Vale.

Dolly seems to approach the generation that has followed her with a suspicion Marge is alert to in her friend, and tries to quell:

> Dolly: I bet she'll get a flat. They do it to get a flat, half of them.

> Marge: Well, she didn't. Girls don't get pregnant to get
> flats, Dolly, they're too stupid.

There is a striking truth in Marge's reply. 'They're too stupid' implies no criticism of the people Dolly has been speaking about – rather, what Marge reminds us of is that the people in question are as lost and immersed in their lives as anyone else, are not enacting a plan or exploiting a loophole. They, like Marge and Dolly, live in a siege, and struggle enough just to get by without laying elaborate plans. Marge is insistent that the people around her, the people being viewed by the play, must be treated as humans, not symbols, and not have any more or anything different expected of them because of the conditions of their lives:

> Marge: Well, you can't expect people to behave better just
>   because they had a tragedy.
> Dolly: Well, you'd think –
> Marge: It seems as if you'd think somehow they'd be
>   elevated and know better.

This is a vital argument of the play. Gill does not use the world he depicts to make a point – his point lies in the depiction of the world, in the insistence that it exists the same as any other. The points are made by us in the bar afterwards. It is in this context that we must approach the anxieties and insecurities of the characters as they resurface – as questions being sincerely asked, not attempts to cast light on a particular class. Annie demonstrates the shorthand reading we could make of this world succinctly when she says, 'No job, well, you know how it is. Hard times.' Her brevity makes a compelling point about reading people reductively as social components – there's very little to say about them when they're treated like indicators. The opportunity for exploration lies in their actual lives, not the newspaper features about them. Shirley, speaking to Billy, argues that stepping away from real and human emotions dulls and kills them: 'You drink because without it you can't feel nothing... You know there's more to you and then you go and have to drink to feel it.' She might as well be talking about the vocabulary of class.

When we address human questions through corollaries, whether alcohol or language, we simplify, we miss or kill the point that wanted making in the first place. Shirley accuses Billy of performing this kind of violence when he refuses to speak to her, when he stays out, when he leaves her isolated and alone: 'You see, you see your cruelty. How you make me cruel, how you reduce me to the cruelty I'm capable of... Look at her, look what you did and now it's too late to stop it.'

Billy, the morning after his domestic with Shirley, seems most deeply immersed in anxiety and uncertainty in this sequence:

> Billy: Why is there love?
> Marge: Oh, Billy.
> Billy: Why do you need it? You can't tell a baby, a little baby, you love it. It wouldn't understand... Oh, you can't only talk to a baby, Marge. You can't just say, 'why are you crying?' You know that. 'What do you want?' We've all tried that. You can't say, 'Tell me what you want, if you stop crying I'll get you what you want', can you? You try getting a baby down with words. Words won't do. Sex don't do it. My feelings, my feelings.

Darkie and Stella also find themselves pulled into an argument about love, as the connections between people are laid open and questioned, the actual feeling below the false flowers or family dinners societies swear by as stand-ins for real interaction:

> Darkie: Look what you're doing, to make me depend on you. I'm not going to get out of this. You ask me for everything, but where are you for me? Where are you when I want you? Not here, not here, you're not here, Mam. What did you do this to me for? You made me like this, caring for you, waiting for you.
> Stella: I am the devil, this is evil. Hell is a place you go to for allowing yourself to suffer. When suffering seems like sin. I try to say my prayers but I can't empty out my mind. It all seems so sinful.

The play's suggestion is, in part, that to begin to pull these problems apart is inherently reductive – they are human conditions, and cannot be reduced to symptoms, causes and solutions. Their source is the anxiety that comes with being alive and the need people feel for other people. To look at them, to give them attention, is the play's action, and the next step in sympathetically engaging with these people is left to the audience watching in the dark. Any alternative, any attempt to label or conclude, is revealed as not only reductive but implicitly dangerous by Annie, when Marge offers an opinion of what it must have been like to live among Jews before the war:

> Marge: Low life they must have seemed.
> Annie: No.

The simple 'no' speaks volumes. Marge's comment is first of all shown to be ridiculous – of course they won't have seemed like low life, they will have seemed simply like life, caught up in the same siege and facing the same limits and problems. There is a greater resonance to that 'no' in the context of a discussion of the war, though, as the implications of the suggestion and the rebuttal are left to hang in the air.

Michael suggests early in the next scene that the audience watching this play belong to a different world to the world in question, with the barbed observation that: 'ethics aren't for us, we just have morals. We're not material, there is no us any more, we don't exist, we're not material.' This is a densely packed idea – Michael further reinforces the idea that an intellectualised, ethical reading of these lives is irrelevant, whilst also implying a distance between the 'us' he invokes and the unmentioned but audibly uncomfortable audience, watching this from the Cottesloe stalls – the 'them' for whom ethical understanding was the reason they came to see a play about this world. The same discomfort is evoked again when Marge says: 'You know when they talk about our children, they don't mean their children.' Her point implies a kind of scorn for the idea of sympathetic understanding, which is made so different by the distance between the world of the political soundbite and the world of Cardiff East, two worlds with very different frames of reference and experience. This is a well rehearsed argument, and Gill lets it play out:

> Marge: Feminism, it's for women with rich husbands and
>   a university degree. It's too good for the working class.
> Tommy: Up the working class.
> Marge: You've got to be in work to be in the working class,
> Tommy. Or available for work.
> Dolly: They say everyone's working class now.
> Marge: Yes. Well, if the junior doctors find it so hard why
>   don't they go over Panasonic for £4.80 an hour?

The same sardonic perspective is invoked by Michael when he observes: 'I heard some rich black singer, some rich American rock singer on about this being the land of slavery. I doubt if some farm labourer, speaking Welsh, living here on this land, had ever heard of slavery, paying his tithes. Or America.'

The scene proceeds to explore the moral framework Michael proposes, which very quickly coalesces around a discussion of faith – unsurprising, as Michael is a priest, but also because, as the discussion plays out, it becomes clear that faith is the moral and social bedrock of this world. Michael begins with a joke about value systems as Dolly pours cold water on the Catholic impulse to guilt:

> Dolly: You have to be careful that it isn't like making a cup
>   of tea with a sense of sin.
> Michael: And you a Catholic. You're a moral relativist,
>   Dolly, you want to watch it. That's what we have a
>   church for, that's what we have churches for, to
>   manage things like that, to teach us what is right and
>   wrong. That's what Radio Four is for.

But this is quickly supplanted by a moving, lucid and simple reading of the tenets of the faith that binds these people together:

> Michael: The essential message of Our Lord, mercy over

justice.
Marge: Love.
Michael: Yes, love next to justice.
Marge: And not pride –
Dolly: and not to judge –
Marge: and love the poor.
Michael: And love the poor and love the poor.

This statement of collective feeling reveals another aspect of this community to us – the sense of cohesion and shared purpose and belonging that holds them together, that has been expressed since the start of the play through the juxtaposition of these lives on the same stage, but is now addressed directly. Michael gestures towards a kind of shared folk memory that has informed him and surely identifies him as belonging to this place above all others when he says:

Michael: I remember things I can't have witnessed. I remember things that can't have happened. The German plane crash.
Annie: It wasn't a German plane. It was a –
Michael: Yes, in the next street.
Annie: It was a Polish airman who took off from the old airport and he crashed, and Charlie pulled him out. He was a hero, Charlie. He saved him.
Marge: Did he?
Annie: The King gave him a medal. The King gave him a medal.

These stories, worn pebble smooth by re-telling, anchor the characters into the same lives in a positive and fulfilling way. They are not only grouped together by income and opportunity, but by values and history. Annie and Michael subside after this exchange into wordless memory:

Annie: Years ago.
Michael: Years ago.

What they fall back into remembering is not said, but the implication in the repetition is that something is shared here. Michael, certainly, feels he belongs to this world: 'I feel I came from this city, I suppose, but I also – I feel like I come from just these few streets.' His perspective is the most eloquently expressed of the scene, and the most overtly political, as he goes on again to invoke the idea of 'us' and 'them' which began the scene, contrasting 'these few streets' and how he feels for them with the rest of the country: 'Perhaps people like us can't feel the conscience of the nation, perhaps that's why they invented the American dream... Nationalism is just a retreat from something that was greater. The poor bloody Welsh, they did it without killing a sodding one. They should have took up arms. No one gives a toss for them, it seems to me.'

Collective feeling becomes the dominant note of the play, as the characters switch to speaking in Welsh, and their experience moves beyond our hearing, in effect (I generalise once more about the Cottesloe audience, but I would expect that most nights, no one knew what was being said at this point). What we see instead is a community connected by language, enclosed by difference from 'us', cohesive though separate from our lives. Following the section in Welsh, we see evening fall and the characters engage in a variety of games, all being played simultaneously on stage: snooker, skittles, bingo show us the characters again all engaged in shared experience, experiences I have previously designated as pale escapes from the siege of their lives but which, nonetheless, we now see give them the same pleasure anyone feels in a game. Returning to our earlier experience of Schubert's 'Ave Maria', we hear the characters singing different songs, several voices laid over each other, and again, we are shown a group of people alive and immersed in living, regardless of anything else that is happening, singing and happy and overflowing the stage with life. Michael, speaking of his faith, says that 'it all became one thing. Where I could put all my feelings, all my confusions about what was going on, all my contradictions.' These games and songs are the same one thing – the shared world into which people pour their lives. The intercutting of scenes accelerates, as Gill writes towards a crescendo, and the play ends with two wordless, moving conclusions, as Neil grabs Tommy's head and kisses him at the same time as Billy gives Shirley a knife, and Shirley knifes Billy. This act of love and the accompanying act of despair – the only real acts of the play, which has seen people sitting and speaking and waiting to sleep, but never acting on their impulses until now, conclude the action of the play, and leave us with two pictures, not of life in one place, but of universally experienced human emotion, expressions of human longing and desire and insecurity and fear, to take away with us into the night.

★

Certain Young Men was first performed at the Almeida Theatre, London, on 21 January 1999 with the following cast:

Stewart – Alec Newman
Michael – John Light
David – Jeremy Northam
Christopher – Andrew Woodall
Andrew – Andrew Lancel
Tony – Peter Sullivan
Robert – Sean Chapman
Terry – Danny Dyer

Directed by Peter Gill
Designed by Nathalie Gibbs
Lighting by Hartley T.A. Kemp
Sound by Frank Bradley
Casting by Toby Whale
Costume Supervisor Charlotte Stuart

★

Certain Young Men, Gill's next play, represented a departure from previous production models, being produced by the Almeida

Theatre rather than the Royal Court or the National Theatre – it was the first of his plays not to have had its first production with one of those two companies. The play, like *Cardiff East*, is of panoramic scope – Gill returned to the subterranean London of *Mean Tears* and even more literally to the London of *In the Blue*, which is re-used as one of the interweaving narrative strands of *Certain Young Men*, slightly rewritten but effectively the same play enclosed within a larger narrative, a broader perspective. Once again, we are presented with graduate students, rent boys and heroin users, as well as with fathers and strugglers – the overall impression is of a group of characters who are struggling with life, and specifically with the difficulty of making meaningful connections with other people in their lives.

The play begins with the restatement of *In the Blue*, and a succinct evocation of the difficulty of connecting with another person. Michael and Stewart are swapping phone numbers, uncertain the numbers will ever be called – 'You probably won't ring anyway' - and the opening image, of the exchange of pieces of paper being a more effective connection than the act of speech between them, which breaks down time and again, made all the more poignant by the fact that the hopeful connection of the exchanged phone number is only going to lead to further failed attempts at speech, establishes a thesis of longing and loneliness that sustains through the play. A moment when Stewart begins to unbuckle his belt seems to offer another possible method of connection, through sex, but the presence of a sleeping flatmate, Lenny, who never wakes or appears in the play but is nonetheless revealed as present in the room, stops them exploring this field of connection. Instead they are left with their attempts at conversation, which break down as we have already seen into Michael's reimaginings, and end with the question 'Are you a student?' – the final line of the scene the most mundane of all, the most commonly heard at parties and hopeless at bridging the distance between these two men. It is sad that the line which is most strongly suggested as what really happened by being the last stated action is the most mundane failure of communication in the whole scene. Michael and Stewart return in Scene Three, and here Gill offers a beautiful picture of failure, reminiscent of the ineloquent exchanges of *Over Gardens Out*:

> Michael: Or...
> *They roll towards each other simultaneously, one tumbling over the other as they meet and end up some distance apart, each lying on his back.*
> Stewart: I like being with you. I do. D'you hear me? You. What about you. Hey.
> *He hurls a book at Michael.*
> Michael: You're beautiful. I know that.

These children's actions, the distance they end up sitting apart, and the unanswered, thrown platitudes, are an extraordinary expression of longing and of an inability to express that longing. The image repeats throughout the play, a dominant motif: in Scene Six, we see Michael crawling towards Stewart on his hands and knees but stopping before he reaches him. Later still, Michael begins to feel ill:

> Michael: Now I feel sick.
> He bends over, his hands on his knees.
> Stewart: No, don't feel sick.

This is another painful exchange. Stewart's exhortation is powerless, a request without authority, because no one can stop someone else feeling sick just by saying so. It is a portrait of the space between the two men, their ineffectual desire to help or affect each other.

Failures of communication have clearly forced the next scene, between David and Christopher, who have just spent the day in Oxford:

> David: I thought you'd look nice in a punt.
> Christopher: I come from Oxford. I didn't go to Oxford.

These two men not quite fighting each other, not quite able to confront an unhappiness that is evident between them, obviously share wider concerns of belonging as well – which Oxford they belong to, for example, and, as we learn through the progress of the scene, whether they belong to each other. The social worlds they belong to (or not) recur as subject matter between them throughout the scene. Christopher jokes about David's template tastes: 'Well I put up with your pictures. The statutory Matisse', as well as suggesting his own sense of not belonging:

> Christopher: I used to work with people who would have gone to a party on the Marchioness. Girls in advertising who eventually wanted to get into films... It was always someone's birthday or leaving party... I was glad.
> David: Of the elbow?
> Christopher: Yes. I was. It meant I didn't have to make a decision.

While in the scene between Michael and Stewart we were able to see Michael's redraftings of his conversations, here we are given access to David and Christopher's internal thoughts, which give a depth and an emotional weight to their half-interactions, as we learn what it is the two men are not quite able to get across:

> David: [*Christopher goes out*]. You think this is it. You think this is... smudge of oil on his cheek. That's the way his hair falls when parted. This is... him. I see him going from startled laughing unbelieving boy to junker-headed sensualist.

David is imprisoned by powerless love and unable to control or communicate his feelings, and the suggestion arises that the exchanges about belonging between the two men are covers for a more essential question – as to whether or not they belong to each other. The frustration Christopher reveals through his own inner monologue seems to suggest that passion and uncertainty as strongly as David's:

> Christopher: I like that play. That play.

> David: What play?
> Christopher: I liked it.
> David: What, that political play?
> Christopher: No, no. That play.
> David: I don't remember.
> Christopher: You do. That play. I want to set fire to him. I
>   want to crash my bike into a moving lorry. Jump off
>   the bridge. Throw him out of a moving taxi. Saved by
>   the bell. Seconds out.

This is a world of negotiations, texts and subtexts, unexpressed desires that turn into awkward half silences between the two men, and an obsession with roles. David is capable of satirising this obsession:

> David: Why does she think that a gluten free diet is the
>   answer to an unhappy child? What's wrong with the
>   child. He's got his imitation Royal Family coat.

This is the same witty voice we encountered in *Mean Tears*, the brilliant young man able to deftly pick out social indicators such as the 'imitation Royal Family coat'. Christopher displays the same skill:

> Christopher: She wants to send him away to school.
> David: Where?
> Christopher: That school for very gifted parents.

This obsession, however, stems from their more personal preoccupation, their questioning of the roles played within a relationship, and the extent to which one person's need for another is limited by their having to play a particular role:

> David: For you I am someone to have laughs and be free
>   with.
> Christopher: Yes.
> David: And free of.

David suffers in the knowledge of the limits of Christopher's feelings for him, the effects of there only being a contained part of Christopher's life where he matters. Later in the play, when Christopher has gone back to Oxford to visit his son, David finds himself needing to tell Christopher: 'I rang you. I exist. When you're there I'm here OK.' This is a succinct and painful evocation of the limits of Christopher's love and the way they hollow out another person. David is also unable to do anything to alter the state of affairs beyond remind and insist – he tolerates the situation he is in instead, apparently incapable of changing it. David is a man affected and limited by his past. In a later scene, he narrates a day spent with his mother, in which they go to a gallery:

> David: I know she wants to see Ophelia Drowning –
> because she's sent me a postcard of it twice. Then we
> have lunch and then a matinee. I couldn't face it.

This 'I couldn't face it', this incapacity, is central to his character. He doesn't even believe himself capable of real incapacity:

> David: I don't think I'm incompetent enough. She prefers
> my brother, who's a hopeless drunk or you because
> you've done something interesting.

Here, he reveals himself to believe that he hasn't, by implication, done anything interesting with his life. He exists in the shadows of other people – of his brother, of Christopher, the 'you' of that passage, and of his mother, whose presence draws him back into a hopeless, powerless schoolboy past he is failing to recover from:

> David: I don't know why I'm being so ungenerous. She's
> a really good woman. It's just seeing her on the train
> always makes me think of going back to school.

Like the characters in *Mean Tears*, David is a man struggling to deal with the drift of adult life – the removal of structure that comes at the end of education, the lack of purpose it is all too easy to feel as a result of that. He is in recovery from his schooldays.

The interest, complexity and life of the relationship between David and Christopher derives from the fact that the imbalance between them is not a neat or soluble one – the see-saw between David and Christopher is not equally off kilter, and this is what makes it difficult to solve, as well as making it true, and like life, and a real love. While David feels a distance between himself and Christopher, Christopher wishes for more of one, and the imbalance between them is laid bare:

> Christopher: Get out of my head. Get out of it. I'm... in and out of you. You... I feel I'm chasing up the motorway the wrong way.

The next pair of characters we encounter are similarly engaged in a not-quite-argument. Andrew comes home late, to find Tony waiting for him:

> Andrew: Why don't you ask me why I'm late?
> Tony: You'll tell me. I don't have to ask you.
> Andrew: Why don't you ask me? Don't you want to know? You angry?

There is both love and aggression in the speech of both men. Andrew, at one level, wants to force Tony into enough of a confrontation that he might be able to perhaps apologise to him – he certainly seems to speak out of a desire to create more speech, of need to connect to another person. But his question is simultaneously a challenge, a distancing attack, which makes it more difficult for Tony to talk to him. So Tony's apparently trusting, reconciliatory response is also a piece of passive-aggressive fencing, a powerplay making it clear he is waiting for Andrew to open up and doesn't feel he should do the running. The two men are not quite connecting, as Andrew goes on to spell out when he talks about their shared evenings:

> Andrew: We'll stay in. You'll read the paper. I'll watch the
> telly. I'll read the paper and you'll watch the telly and
> then we both might watch the telly.

Tony, similarly aware of this failure to connect, attempts to raise it as an issue:

> Tony: You can't let go – can you? Can you though? You
> won't let it happen between us. There's all the outside,
> you've got to bring it home. I'm tired of all the outside.

Like the other pairings before them, Andrew and Tony are locked into a connection that doesn't quite satisfy either of them, but which they undoubtedly recognise as essential, and existing:

> Andrew: When through all the thoughts I clear a path I
> think I'm alive. This is alright. This is OK. The light in
> the sky reflected as my eyes brim. Then this almost...
> feeling. I think of you. I have to love you. I know I
> must.

The dissatisfaction for Andrew extends beyond the failings of his connection with Tony. Andrew is one of the more eloquent characters Gill has written, capable of the same eviscerations practised by the characters in *Mean Tears* and acute in his observations of the world around him. His dissatisfaction with his life is beautifully drawn:

> Andrew: Look at this barbie. I got a soap dish. That's me.
> Plastic! Cool. Plastic toast rack. Look at this plate, that
> record. Tape for the car. Tape for the car. Annie
> Lennox. The Tourists.
> Tony: What's wrong with it?
> Andrew: That's not life. That's getting a life, that is. Get a
> life. I don't want a life. Life happens between those
> things.

As well as his dissatisfaction with homogenised, commodified life, Andrew feels dissatisfaction with gay life: 'I don't want all this... Gay. Gay this, gay that.' This is a dissatisfaction which Andrew expresses in greater depth three scenes later, in a two hander with a new character, Robert, who is as eloquent as Andrew in expressing the pale, prescriptive conformity of gay life. This scene, too, begins with an evasive entrance from Andrew:

> Robert: Did you walk into a door?
> Andrew: Yeah. Something like that.

Andrew then revisits the subject he has previously discussed with Tony, feeling all the more false and staged in his 'got' life for being a gay man in a gay relationship: 'What are two men doing living together faking all the stupidities of a fake straight relationship, what's that all about?... I don't want to be an imitation of an imitation.' His conclusions about gay life are dismissive:

> Andrew: That's gay culture. That's about the size of it.
>   Don't laugh. The make of your underpants.
> Robert: Oh I don't...
> Andrew: Well what else. What else has come out of gay
>   culture? Discos. Body fascism. Is there a gay commu-
>   nity?

Robert's response to this, however, complicates and develops the picture, as the two men begin to engage more constructively with the actual subject of Andrew's dissatisfaction, rather than simply the object he has chosen to locate it in:

> Robert: Well in so far as gay men oppress themselves,
>   there's very like what you call a gay community. I can't
>   imagine there's been much of a call for a homeland
>   though... But you're searching for a solution. What if
>   there is no solution to anything.

Robert begins to subtly question the existence of this 'real life' Andrew seems to hold some hope of when he damns by comparison the purchased life spent listening to Annie Lennox and The Transports that most people, as he sees it, fall into. Robert proposes a gentle scepticism about whether there is such a 'real life', by pointing out to Andrew the binary nature of his thinking, his yearning for solutions, and then proceeding to chip away at the idea of it being possible to belong to anything, to feel at home and genuinely present in any world:

> Robert: Have you ever been to Pride?
> Andrew: No. I wanted to go. He wouldn't, see. To see what it's like.
> Robert: Well you should go the once. I only went the once. But it's not me. But then neither is the Last Night of the Proms. So you can't go by me. I wouldn't like the Highland Games. Or the County show. Or the Welsh National Eisteddfod. Or St Patrick's Day in New York. Or an Orange March. Or the Notting Hill Carnival. Or Badminton or the Cup Final. I'm not a great fan of the British Legion. But being queer can be a project like anything else.

Robert speaks about himself, but he is also removing Andrew's certainties. His suggestion, when he speaks about projects, is that all life and all happiness is an elective decision one takes, a process one engages in, not a real life it is possible to discover and fall into, an emotional homeland. His argument is that any more abstract theory is fanciful: 'You want to know why you're with someone. Don't think there's much more to it than knowing who you're spending the weekend with or Easter or Bank Holidays. It's someone to share the torture with. What's the alternative? That's what most people have concluded... people aren't in couples for the general good. I don't see pair bonding as some predetermined absolute.'

This argument does not preclude Robert from feeling the same impulse to question the limits of his life, as Andrew does. He recognises the dissatisfaction that underpins Andrew's life, and proposes it as a basic human state: 'It's to do with a struggle that everyone has with the fact of gender. The anger of all of us at being biologically sorted. Look at straight men. Most straight men are male impersonators.' As this last comment suggests, he also reads the world around him with the same deconstructive detachment as Andrew, recognising in it the limiting elements of needing to take on these projects as a way of filling your life: 'these are prescriptive times. There are choices and they want you to make them. For some you've got to wear a suit or at least a jacket. Have what they call a partner. Now there's a word. There's a word for the market place.' But he suggests that these prescriptions are necessary evils for taking a place in the world, for taking part:

> Robert: The price you have to pay for being comfortable.
> Andrew: I don't want to take part.
> Robert: Well join the radical wing of the movement. Where to be really queer you have to have someone nail your foreskin to a piece of wood and generally kick up a bit of a fuss. All this sounds much better in the original French... I think queers are still ultimately transgressive... The unkennelled seeking out of differ-ence. But in English it all takes on a homely air.

His joke about rebellion, of course, is that it is as predictable and prescribed as conformity, just as being gay is as prescriptive and limiting as being straight: 'We're just another niche in the market... Well able and willing to be neutralised. Sentimental, silly, frivolous, a bit of a laugh, very sympathetic listeners.' *Certain Young Men* is, in part, a wry exploration of these roles and performativities. In the scenes between David and Christopher there are some very 'Grim Up North London' exchanges, with the two men aware of the roles they are playing, and playing them anyway:

> David: Not herbal tea. Not herbal tea.
> Christopher: Yes herbal tea. It's quite nice.
> David: What's it called?
> Christopher: Happy Apple.

The play's final pair of characters are then introduced, and here, in the character of a boy called Terry, a different element enters the play. Terry was played in the Almeida production by a young Danny Dyer, who drew extraordinary responses from critics, the public and the rest of the company with his perform-ance. Andrew Woodall describes watching Dyer with something akin to dismay, saying that the group of trained and experienced actors who made up the rest of the company (Dyer had not gone to drama school) felt like they might as well go home having seen his work. Terry is a dream of a part – a vulnerable, unselfcon-scious boy, sexually promiscuous, emotionally desperate, a liar – he claims in quick succession 'I never went to school. I never went to school, never. Honest. I didn't', then 'I went to boarding school. I did'. He is incapable of disguising his emotions – upon being rejected by Andrew, he resorts to playground ineloquence to cover his hurt: 'well, yeah, I'll fuck off then. Fuck off then you. Alright. Fuck off. You don't know nothing, you don't. I'm fucking off. Fuck you.' He displays an extraordinary sincerity and emotional simplicity, which makes him seem very unguarded:

> Terry: Girls are all OK. Aren't they. No. I'm like, well, you fuck a girl easier, like. Obvious. But blokes suck cock better, don't they? Funny that, innit?... I like blokes. I know more about geezers. Girls are all over you. I've always been round blokes. Most of the girls I know wear knickers to keep their ankles warm... I know a girl I like. But she's chirping all the time.

This lack of self-consciousness also manifests itself as an extraordinary naivety: 'If it's going to get you, it's going to get you. Next time I'll bring loads of condoms.' His naivety is poignant for having been formed, in part, by the neglect of the society around him – no one has impressed upon him strongly enough that 'next time' isn't the right time to bring condoms. His aspirations, similarly, his worldview, are damaged by the world he lives in:

> Terry: What could I be?

Andrew: Lots of things.
Terry: I could be a TV chef. I like cooking. Or have a chat
   show – like Montel. Or I could be in a boy band. Yeah.

This is a child without role models, turning to the television for something to want. The suggestion emerges as he speaks that, more than simply not being sufficiently encouraged by his family, he has in fact been abused by his father: 'My fucking father. That's all right though, innit. Keep it in the family.' This background warps him into statements that seem violently unhealthy – speaking again of paedophiles, he says, 'they're just like anyone else.' But I would propose there is also an extraordinary clear-sightedness in this, which is what makes Terry so captivating – unencumbered, or unprotected, by context, he speaks as he finds. I'm sure if you were to sit unknowingly across a table from a paedophile, they would indeed seem just like anyone else. But it takes a naivety, a childlike reading of the world, to be able to observe that.

Terry is, above all, a desperately lonely and vulnerable boy, who expresses in terms as simple and direct as Michael and Stewart's dumbshows the dominant subject of *Certain Young Men* – the need people feel for each other.

Terry: No. I don't do drugs... I don't drink... the weekend.
   You know, that's all. I'd like to kiss you. I would.
   Straight. I would. Do you want me to fuck you? Do you
   want to fuck me? I don't mind. I'm coming down. I'm
   feeling very, you know, like... I'd like to see you. Can I
   see you?
Andrew: You are seeing me.
Terry: Come off it.
Andrew: Yeah. You can see me. But you won't come
   round.
Terry: If I don't come round, you'll know you can never
   trust me again. Come on.

The difference here is that Terry's medium is verbal – he is the spoken expression of the idea of the play, as well as its clearest visual picture of human vulnerability. Again, his youthfulness is key to his being able to express what the other characters dance around – it takes a young boy, still growing out of asking girls 'will you go out with me', to identify the sense of belonging all the characters seek. Andrew immediately recognises and defends against what Terry wants – to 'see' him, what you sometimes hear called 'be with' him, the strange default 'in a relationship' state which Terry is trying to get to, is really wanting when he asks Andrew whether he wants to kiss him or fuck him.

What Terry is talking about, of course – and what *Certain Young Men* is talking about – is love, a word that is not used until we are some time immersed in the action of the play when Stewart says to Michael in Scene Twelve, 'Do you love me? You love every fucker you do.' Terry is the catalyst for this subject's broaching. Moving between different characters in the play and connecting up the isolated worlds and two-handers that have so far populated the stage, he is constantly broaching the subject no one else can bring up:

Terry: I don't know what I'm going to do. I been on the rob again. I ain't got no money. I ain't got no one. I ain't got nowhere.
Andrew: Are you sleeping?
Terry: Here and there.
Andrew: This is no good. Honest. I'm sorry.
Terry: I ain't got no one. I'd like to have you. I'd like to be with you. Don't get rid of me. You want me to go.

The desperate sadness of Andrew's silence during that long last line is upsetting. Andrew finds himself powerless to ease the pain in Terry, to do any more than advise that he get some sleep. Andrew is besieged by need he can do nothing about, experiencing it from Tony as well, and responding by saying: 'I'm angry about what I can't change and what it is you still find in me... I'm so tired of making sense of the senseless.' Tony responds by saying to him, 'please, Andrew. I'm lonely. I'm lonely without you', the first admission of loneliness in a play filled with lonely people, coming even later than the first reference to love. Andrew refuses to let this narrative of loneliness and loving absorb him, to become part of someone's project, to become part of a gay imitation of a fake straight relationship, and so the longing that forces these scenes goes unresolved.

David and Christopher, who have been negotiating around love in the form of Christopher's child (the inanimate 'bundle' not appearing on stage here, but just as potent a symbol as it has been in previous of Gill's plays) also begin to address the need they have for each other more directly as the play progresses:

> Christopher: You're the most exciting person I've ever met. And the most exhausting. When you're interested, you really are interested. You never forget anything I've ever said about myself – you make me feel I belong to you in some way. As though I'm part of you and I don't like it. Because. Well, it's as though I'm some extension of. That I'm some territory you know very well and are angry at losing... your jealousy is very frightening because it makes me feel I don't exist.

These are the effects of love – effects we have seen before in *Small Change*, and *Mean Tears*, and which render Christopher powerless, incapable of controlling his own life because he finds it necessary to exist in the context of someone else. The territory he speaks of, which I have been calling the distance between them, is not space he can take for himself because he does not have control over his emotional state.

This contested territory, where *Certain Young Men* takes place, is an uncertain place of miscommunications and missed connections. Stewart and Michael try to reach each other across it but can't:

> Michael: Or...
> Stewart: We'll be all right.
> Michael: Or...
> Stewart: What do you want?
> Michael: Or...
> Stewart: Just tell me!

Because they cannot connect successfully with the thing most important to them, they are lost instead in the same drift David experiences, the same purposelessness and powerlessness:

> Michael: Or...
> Stewart: I don't know what I'm doing here.

Gill ends the play with a final attempt by the two men to reach each other, which reduces, once again, to inanimate struggling between them. Here, though, he juxtaposes this established picture with the vulnerable and moving image he has made out of Terry, who is seen looking in through a window, alone, shouting for someone else, lonely and isolated like Michael and Stewart, but, where they are locked into a reciprocal exchange, Terry is caught in solitude, alone with his nose to the glass.

> Michael: Or...
> Stewart: Come on.
> *Stewart pulls Michael by the arm.*
> Michael: No.
> Stewart: Yes. Come on. Come on. Come on!
> Michael: No.
> Stewart: Come on.
> *There is a violent struggle between Michael and Stewart during which Terry stands and calls as at a window.*
> Terry: Are you in? Let me in. Let me in. Are you in? Let me in, let me in. Let me in.
> *Michael and Stewart have stopped struggling.*
> Stewart: It's all right.
> Do you want to leave it then?

Stewart's final suggestion is rendered hopeless by the presence of Terry – a stark visual reminder that being alone would solve nothing, just as being with someone else solves nothing. As Andrew has insisted through the play, there is no sense to be made out of these situations, all sense and structure overlaid over human beings is as artificial and unimportant as what kind of underpants you wear. There is only vulnerability, and the state of suffering or being in recovery which the experience of life can sometimes resemble. *Certain Young Men* is a masterpiece; a moving and extraordinary exploration of love, longing, and human need that resolves nothing, and expresses that it does so because there is nothing to resolve – there is just life, happening around us and before us on the stage.

7. REMEMBRANCE OF FORMER THINGS
THE YORK REALIST, ANOTHER DOOR CLOSED,
VERSAILLES

T he *York Realist* received its world premiere on 15 November 2001 at The Lowry, Salford Quays, with the following cast:

George – Lloyd Owen
John – Richard Coyle
George and Barbara's Mother – Anne Reid
Barbara – Caroline O'Neill
Arthur – Ian Mercer
Doreen – Wendy Nottingham
Jack – Felix Bell

Directed by Peter Gill
Designed by William Dudley
Lighting Designer: Hartley T.A. Kemp
Composer: Terry Davies
Assistant Director: Josie Rourke
Dialect Coach: Jeanette Nelson
Casting Director: Toby Whale

★

Gill's next play after *Certain Young Men* was marked by a striking change in aesthetic – after thirty years of suggesting in his opening stage directions that his plays should be presented on a practically bare stage, *The York Realist* asked for a 1960s farm labourer's cottage in Yorkshire to be depicted on the stage. This apparently radical departure can, however, be read as a return to an older aesthetic which Gill had stripped away for most of his career. The fully realised interior is a rural counterpart to Mrs Shannon's back-to-back grate in *The Sleepers Den*, and, perhaps more significantly, to the minute 'high Victorian' naturalism of Gill's Lawrence productions – the play is steeped in Lawrence, as any reader of *Sons and Lovers* will instantly recognise. *The York Realist* is a loving re-engagement with the Lawrentian aesthetic, that consciously echoes those plays on many levels – the burning of the bread in *A Collier's Friday Night* is consciously invoked in *The York Realist* when the two boys at the centre of the play go out without doing the washing up, while the play's cast – a family, crossing several generations and living in several houses, spread so far as to be a focused portrait of a whole community – recall Lawrence's nuanced studies of families in his plays.

That being said, *The York Realist* does certainly have lead roles, in the form of George and John, a Yorkshire farm labourer and a young theatre director from London who meet on a production of the York mystery plays which John is assistant directing and which George has been encouraged to take part in by Doreen, a woman who clearly has designs of marriage on him. As in Lawrence, this is no secret – everything is known in the world of *The York Realist*, the small community in rural Yorkshire where secrets are not kept, but are not spoken either, instead being negotiated around. In George and John, Gill returns to that dominant theme in his work, relationships between men and the distances that are uncrossable within and between them. In *Certain Young Men* these distances were opened up by love, or children, or age, or interest, but here Gill revisits ground previously covered in *Small Change* by using this relationship to examine the incompatibility of lifestyles – this time of the Yorkshire farmer and the London artist, while in *Small Change* it was the London artist and the Cardiff worker. In *Small Change*, the autobiographical suggestion was difficult to resist – Gill, son of a Cardiff docker and exile from his history in the London art scene, could be read in Gerard's agonised, painstaking monologues and cataloguing of the world he revisits as he revisits Cardiff and his past. In *The York Realist* any autobiographical element is more deftly disguised, as the play's study of exile does not extend to observing a man who returns to somewhere he no longer feels at home – it is a study of people confronting worlds they can never belong to. The exiling in the play has more to do with Moses, shown the kingdom he will never set foot in, as the two men find themselves unable to live in the worlds they would like to – which is to say, with each other. They are too far apart, their experiences dividing them irresolvably, as the play shows.

As in *Small Change*, the impulse that prompts the play is a return, which, as in that earlier play, prompts a memory. This act of remembering, however, acts as a chiastic envelope around the play rather than a constant thread that runs through it, a complicating and ironising lens through which we view an otherwise linear narrative. At the outset of *The York Realist*, John comes back to George's cottage some time after he last visited it, compelled to see George as the play he is directing visits York. Their opening exchanges show us much of what has happened between them. The play begins with them both struggling to speak to each other:

> George: Well.
> John: Yes.
> George: Aye.
> John: Yeah...
> George: Well then. Mm... Yeah... Come in.

Their exchanges begin to excavate a history between them. It is clear John has learned to drive since he last visited George, and that he has stayed with him in the past:

> George: You couldn't stay here so easy now. Could you?
> John: No. No. No.
> George: You wouldn't have the excuse of the bus with the car.
> John: We wouldn't.
> George: What?
> John: Have the excuse.
> George: No. Aye, if you stayed here now you could have a proper bath.

It is also made painfully clear with that final line that some kind of longing is at play between the two men. George reveals himself to be swayed by John's opinions even in his absence:

> George: Yes, they offered to take the range out. I wouldn't
>   let them.
> John: Oh.
> George: You said you liked it.

This, accompanied by John driving out to see him, establishes a portrait of two men who are living with each other in mind, if not in body. We learn that George is not living with anyone else – his mother has died, apparently since John last visited as well. And then the play's structure complicates, as, a page after this news reaches us, George's mother walks onto the stage.

We then watch as two time periods exist simultaneously onstage, both possibly visible to George, although Gill does not make this clear with his stage directions. The overlapping stories, one apparently taking place in the past, as we know the mother has died and so cannot be in the house now or in the future, battle against each other for a moment in a densely written three-hander:

> Mother: Do you want a clean shirt, George?
> John: I'm going to the car.
> George: What?
> Mother: Do you want a clean shirt?
> John: I'm going to get something from the car.
> Mother: George.
> John: George.
> George: What?

Then John vacates the stage, and, until the end of the play, we do not see that John or that George onstage again – the whole narrative is pitched back to the first time they met, and the opening of the play has been revealed as a framing device rather than the actual story. The short exchange above recalls some of the overlapping calls from the mothers to the sons and back in

Small Change, but *TheYork Realist* does not subsequently proceed
to expand these clashes and collages – instead, we follow a linear
narrative to an end, returning to the 'present' of John's return to
George after the death of his mother only at the close of the play.

The master of using chiastic envelopes to ironise his work and
give poignancy and layered meaning to events is Chaucer.
Almost all Chaucer's writing uses this device in some way – he
never just tells a story, but sets up a framework within which
stories are told which cohere those smaller narratives, give them
weight, give them more meaning than the simple surface of the
tales themselves. The most famous example of this, of course, is
the Canterbury pilgrimage – but there are, I think, more deftly
woven instances. The heartbroken, doubting narrator of *Troilus
and Criseyde* renders that story moving and immediate for a
reader by turning the whole tragedy of the Trojan war into a way
for a scribe sitting at a desk in the middle ages to express the fact
that he experiences life as a journey in a boat on open seas, being
tossed to and fro by the waves – one of the favourite metaphors
for the experience of living from the Exeter Book to F. Scott
Fitzgerald. When we read that poem we do not read a Greek
myth, but a storyteller who is excising or at least engaging the
complexities of his own psyche through the telling of that particular tale. (Chaucer further complicates the story by inventing a
fictional source author, Lollius, who the 'narrator' figure is translating, and of course by hovering over the text himself, another
layer of authorial presence that further complicates the picture
The *Book of the Duchess* is a subtle and intricate masterpiece in
which Chaucer establishes a character who is unhappy for a
reason he is unable to express, but who is then able to access and
express sideways the source of his unhappiness through the
narrative of the dream he has in the main body of the text. A
great number of narrative devices which were assessed as innova-
tive during the course of the twentieth century can be found in
Chaucer. He seems to have had a mind which worked in a particularly formally inventive way – what Isaiah Berlin would have
called the mind of a fox rather than a hedgehog, filled with
myriad small ideas he had the ingenuity to fit together into stories

like panes of stained glass. The repeating narrative structures in his work – primarily the chiastic envelope which renders the subsequent story moving – seem to have come naturally to him, surface evidence of the way his neural pathways evolved to structure a narrative. Just as Gill's formal invention is perhaps more accurately diagnosed as just being the way he writes, rather than something carefully formulated – a preconscious patterning he could not but adhere to because it is an expression of his self. His slightly more structured and shaped form for *The York Realist*, however, has a Chaucerian look to it. Gill's work is at one level a sustained analysis of the way memory works. On occasion this leads to the literal replication of remembering processes on the stage – here, he studies the effects memory can have on a person. Seeing the two men, tense with their reunion on stage, the only way Gill is able to explain and express that tension, like the dream in *The Book of the Duchess*, is to plunge them back into their own dream of the past. Where Chaucer accesses emotion through allegory, Gill shows how George and John got to the present day of the story through opening up the past to us, showing the process that brought them to this pass.

The story Gill proceeds to tell begins as one between a mother and a son living in the same house. We are introduced into an intimate and private world with a piece of beautiful stage-craft – George, not wanting to change his trousers in front of his mother, is left alone on stage – 'I'll save your modesty and get your dinner' – and changes them in a privacy and solitude in which the audience are enlisted, or on which they are allowed to spy. We are immediately made complicit in this small and enclosed world, this story. The mother then returns to ask George:

> Mother: What happened to your play? You haven't been
> going to your play. Isn't it tonight you go?

George, apparently, has been cast in a play but has not attended rehearsals. He is not forthcoming in his response to his mother's question – and indeed, when his sister Barbara enters

the stage shortly afterwards, it becomes clear he is rarely forthcoming. The two women talk naturally and comfortably over his
head about his not marrying, and the fact that Doreen, dropping
an apparently heavy hint, has made him a pie. As well as talking
around and over the subject of George, they negotiate round
each other in speech, needling without ever confronting on the
subject of Barbara's son:

> Mother: He's in with some bad uns on that estate. That's
> what it'll be. I couldn't live down there.
> Barbara: Well, I wouldn't like to live stuck up here again, I
> can tell you, Mother, like you, without a bath and a
> lavatory outside.

The two women take the opportunity to re-rehearse established grievances with one another's lives, prompted by the excuse
of the boy. This is, on one level, a display of bitterness and animos-
ity – but the subject they negotiate round here, the fact that
Barbara has left the cottages on the hill where George and his
mother still live and gone to live on the estate, has an emblematic,
symbolic look as well – they are symptomatic of a wider life
choice, a movement away from an old way of living to a new one,
a rejection or escape by Barbara, a sense of abandonment from
the mother, and, in the continuing bitterness surrounding the
subject, a sense of continuing connection and need. The things
people don't really care about aren't worth continuing to bring up,
after all, so what is laid bare is a space between Barbara and her
mother, which both seem aware of, and which both have chosen
to coalesce around the choice of home each woman has made.

The evening draws on, patterned similarly to the lives of so
many of Gill's other characters – the Mother tells her family
'Doreen's calling for me later. I promised her I'd go to fellowship
with her. I don't feel up to it', and the world of faith and nerves
is re-established before us once more – until a new arrival
disrupts it. For the second time in the play but the first time in
the chronological narrative of the story, John walks into the
house, looking for George because he hasn't attended rehearsals.
This is the intrusion that prompts the narrative of the play: John's

journey out on the bus to find George, perhaps out of concern for his play, but surely more out of interest in George. The two men are quickly left alone as the women take their cues and leave – their understanding of George, the man at the centre of this cast, will be revealed later in the story to be subtle and complete enough to underline the tact and delicacy with which this community, this family, understand all that goes on in their small, enclosed locality and negotiate around it. The two then share some pleasantries about the play, an opportunity for Gill to lightly send up his world and his craft when George says 'I like Peter. Very interesting man. Doesn't put himself out much, does he? But when he stirs himself he can put his finger on it, can't he... 'Is it an action'?' Before certain traps that have already been laid in Gill's intricately structured play begin to close on us. We see the moment George refers back to, apparently given so much weight by memory, when he proposes removing the fireplace:

> John: I like that. [*Points to the fireplace*].
> George: Want to take it out, that.
> John: No, don't. I'm sorry. It's... I like it.
> George: Not what my mother says.

A tug of war which is at the centre of George and at the centre of the play is established in this final line – between the man he discovers he loves, and the mother he has loved all his life. It is a competition that divides him and renders him incapable of action. By the end of the story we see he is swaying towards John by not taking the fireplace out – but that is a decision he cannot finally make any more because the death of his mother has effectively made the choice impossible, tying him at some level into the life of his home and his history for good. George's closeness to his mother, which will see him stay in Yorkshire when John leaves, which sees him as confounded as Hamlet or Macbeth in his indecision as to which world to live in, condemning him not to live fully in either, is one of the insurmountable barriers between George and John, a symbol around which, like Barbara's house, the two men are able to organise the more general impossibility of living in the same worlds as one another.

The extent to which these worlds are different is measured in part by how beautiful and strange John finds the place to be:

> George: You like it up here, then?
> John: Beautiful.
> George: I'm used to it, me.

John confronts this refusal in the locals to see the world around them as extraordinary throughout the play:

> John: This is a nice cottage, too. How old is it, do you think?
> Mother: Must be old.

All this off-handedness might well just be bluff pretence, but it is also the product of living in a place for a long time and forgetting its qualities as an unusual life becomes habitual. In the film *Local Hero*, a Russian ship's captain explains the attitudes of a village to their locality with the words 'you can't eat scenery', and later in the play we learn that as well as living in a beautiful place, George and his Mother live a serf-like existence, leasing their cottages from an employer who doesn't even own the land he pays them to farm, which is the property of a man who lives in the town and occasionally comes out to hunt – it's this practicality, together with familiarity, which numbs George and his Mother to what John sees in their world, which is the different, the extraordinary, the beautiful. This world they live in is also a disappearing world, a reality that is being effaced by the council estate down the hill and the spread of urban Yorkshire. The cottage next to George's, once occupied by Barbara, now stands empty, and we realise he and his mother are the only people living out in this 'beautiful' isolation – forgotten, perhaps passed over by the march of everything around them. The isolation of the cottage, its difference from the world around it, is revisited in the play's second scene when the characters discuss the Mystery Plays and Jack, Barbara's son, asks: 'Was there a farm labourer's play?' John's offhand reply, 'It was all done in the town', has profound implications for the world on stage – a place outside

history, that has been forgotten and ignored before, just as it is
being forgotten and ignored again now as people move away
from it. The scene ends with George and John going out to
explore this empty landscape together. Neither man has
suggested anything of the sort yet, but Gill's ironising opening
section means we already know John is going to miss his bus.

The play's second scene begins with Doreen and the Mother
returning to the house to find that Jack, Barbara's son, is hiding
in the kitchen eating biscuits. They come across the unwashed
pots and pans George had promised in the previous scene he
would finish cleaning – a device surely intended to evoke
Lawrence, and another moment when it becomes necessary for
the Mother and Doreen to negotiate round George, who has
forgotten that he didn't get round to them. When George and
John return to the cottage, Doreen recounts the reading for the
evening that she and George's Mother have just heard:

> 'There shall be no remembrance of former things.
> Neither shall there be any remembrance of things that are
> to come with those who come after.'

George uses this as an occasion for a joke –

> George: Oh aye. What do you take that to mean, mother?
> Mother: You shut up, you. I think that was very interest-
> ing.
> George: 'Come unto him all ye that labour.' That's what I
> like to hear.

The recounting of the reading is also, however, a striking
foregrounding of the underlying thematic preoccupation with
memory within the play. It addresses the pathetic destiny of the
world we are watching on stage in the grand scheme of social
progress – this disappearing world George and John have just
been exploring, which will surely be forgotten by the world
around it. This is made more poignant by the ironising envelope
of memory around the story, isolating George, whose memory of
this time is torturing him now as it plays out as a remembered

event in the present day of the play.

It seems that the Mother, along with others in the area, may well be attracted by this idea of forgetfulness:

> Mother: You know Mrs Dorset. Lives by you, Doreen. They had old china. Lustreware. Staffordshire figures. Beautiful old stuff. Do you know, when her mother died she smashed it all with a hammer. Got rid of it all. Everything. Got rid of the old furniture. Got rid of the brass. Chopped up the dresser. Sick of all the years washing and polishing. I don't blame her.

The experience of what John sees as charming as a tyrannous influence again returns us to the practicality of the characters who live here – but it exposes a more existential aspect to their dissatisfaction as well. As Mrs Shannon in *The Sleepers Den* is unable to bear the parameters and limits of her own life, so Mrs Dorset here, with the sympathy of the Mother, appears to reject hers. The rage comes from having been limited, having had one life that took one shape, rather than simply the specific limits. It is the idea over the detail that leads to this act of violence.

The scene ends with most of the characters departing, the Mother going to bed, and George forcing a decision from John:

> George: He missed the bus half-hour ago.
> Mother: He never did.
> George: Yeah. Last one's earlier than we thought.

This is quickly followed by:

> John: Have I missed the bus?
> George: I don't know, have you?
> John: Have I?
> George: There's one more. She doesn't know.
> John: Well.
> George: Yes. Your eyes are so bright.

With this last line, George brings into conversation the unspoken attraction that has lain between the two men all this time, made explicit by Gill's framing scene. John tries to put off the resolution of this question, talking again about how strange he finds the world he has stepped into:

> John: It's as you expect it and at the same time it isn't...
> It's all at odds... It puzzled me. Just as you thought it
> would be and yet not. I don't know.

George, again displaying his pragmatism but suggesting there is some other element at play in John's appreciation of his world, a romanticism that may be a product of his background, deflects this with:

> George: You can see what I can't see. Why did you throw
> away the flowers you picked?
> John: Felt silly.
> George: No.
> John: Well, then.
> George: Aye.
> John: What? Oh.
> George: Aye. [Goes towards John].
> John: No.
> George: Sh.
> John: I don't know.

He steers the situation towards its inevitable ending when he goes to the kitchen and returns with a tub of Vaseline:

> John: What's that for?
> George: Vaseline. Be prepared.
> John: No.
> George: Yeah.
> John: Will you come to rehearsals.
> George: That depends on you. Come on.
> John: What about the noise?
> George: You noisy, are you?
> John: Don't be vulgar.

With that the two men disappear to George's room, and the scene closes.

The play's third scene takes place after the opening performance of the York Mystery plays. The family, including Barbara's husband Arthur, return to the cottage, discussing the evening's events:

> Arthur: That was clever how they got him down off that cross. One minute he was up there. The next thing he's facing out the Devil. I never saw him get down. Did you?

There is pleasure to be got from the assimilation of these stories into the lives and languages of these characters. This, for me, is when theatre is most interesting: in the bars or cars or living rooms after a show, when people talk of Jesus 'facing out the Devil', giving a life of their own to the pictures. What a picture wakes in the mind of the individual observer seems to me to be far more fascinating and socially useful than the quality or subtlety of the picture itself (though the quality and subtlety of the original image will of course enrich the response). So as we see Doreen and Jack grapple with how to accommodate Christ into their homes:

> Doreen: All very Yorkshire.
> Jack: Jesus Christ wasn't Yorkshire.

We see theatre performing its essential function – to wake people up; to make people think of their lives. For me a piece of art is successful if it sends me away wanting to do something about my own life, to call a relative or a friend or try harder at something, to support a cause or improve something I care about. It is of value to me if it wakes me up. Whether the York mystery plays have quite done that to this family is unclear – these are passing engagements with what they have seen, not a long conversation – but they are engagements nonetheless, and so I suspect this could be called a successful evening. It is certainly a very attractive thing to put on a stage, the function of a play examined, a relatively rarely presented event.

John and George then return to the cottage as well, and we learn that John wasn't George's first (as we might have guessed from his thinking to bring the Vaseline), but that George has not continued any kind of relationship with the other man he has slept with: 'he thinks it never happened. I got on with it.' The two men then begin to engage with the problem, always looming for theatrical hook-ups once a play has opened, of what they're going to do come the end of the run. John is returning to London now the show has opened, and both are clearly uncertain as to the future:

> George: Is this going to be it when you go?
> John: Come on, why should it? You can come down to see
> me. Write to me.
> George: Aye. I'm a great letter-writer, me.

It might in fact be fairer to say that George, rather than being uncertain, is in fact resigned to an end to this affair. John attempts to sway him, asking him to come to London with him, but knows and admits that George will not leave his mother alone. George, defensive about this, nonetheless agrees with him:

> George: It's you always delving into things. I can't leave
> her now, can I? Well, can I? Aye? Whatever you say the
> reason is. Can I?

The separation takes place because of George's mother – unable to leave her, he decides to stay. It is not until the fourth scene of the play that this simple impossibility is complicated by his mother's death.

The fourth scene takes place immediately after George's mother's funeral. George has returned to the cottage, and is visited by Doreen, who seeks to comfort him – an attempt George bluntly rebuffs:

> Doreen: They all mean well, George.
> George: Course they all mean well. I know that. But

what's that mean to me? Nothing. Nothing. All them
flowers. Waste of brass.

George's bleak insistence that the funeral has been meaningless is painful to encounter, a kind of violence done to Doreen as
she tries to comfort him but also an insistence on the value of his
mother's life over and above every dressing that might be put on
the end of it as consolation when nothing will suitably console the
grieving son. Doreen, in this scene, emerges as a beautiful
Chekhovian portrait. She might be Sonia in *Uncle Vanya* when
she says:

> Doreen: There's no comforting you. I can't comfort you,
>   can I? I can't. Oh dear. I didn't mean to carry on like
>   this. I just want you to take care of yourself.

Gill's relationship with *The Cherry Orchard* as translator and
director seems to achieve its fullest written synthesis here, as we
surely watch a Yorkshire version of the scene where Lopakhin
and Varya are unable to speak to each other. Doreen, defeated by
George's coldness and closedness, is then succeeded in the
cottage by Barbara, offering a more businesslike encouragement
to the still stubbornly broken George:

> Barbara: We'll have to sort her things.
> George: She didn't have anything.
> Barbara: No. But some of her clothes, some poor old
>   people could do with them. That coat you bought her
>   last winter. Doreen'll know someone. She never got the
>   wear of it.

There is great poignancy in this charity, in this isolated
cottage far from anywhere, stemming from Barbara's insistence
on this most Christian of qualities and her failure to realise that
the 'poor old people' she imagines are probably no worse off than
her own mother, and what she is proposing is the recycling of
things through a single, lowly class. 'Things' then take on a
growing significance through the scene, as George discovers his

mother's savings book:

> George: Look at this. [He takes a box from the dresser].
> Barbara: What?
> George: Her savings book.
> Barbara looks in the book.
> Barbara: Nothing in it. What did she keep it for?
> George: I don't know. It was in here with birth certificates
>   and hat – her marriage lines.
> Barbara: Just a penny in to keep it open.
> George: There's her wedding ring. You have it now.
> Barbara: You keep it.
> George: I don't want anything.
> Barbara: You know you don't have to stay. You can do
>   what you like now.
> George: Aye.

The departure of the Mother leaves George with only her possessions, with only inanimate things to remember her by. They become significant, numinous, and yet stubbornly opaque – their meanings and significances will not unfold themselves to him, he cannot understand the savings book, and he can know what the wedding ring meant, but only as symbol, not as vivid, lived memory. The inheritance of this ring is particularly eloquent – a first reference to George's father, it is also the passing on of the act of remembering those who have gone.

This, we are forced to confront, is what a life eventually amounts to – these few possessions left behind after death, a cottage past its time, a wedding ring orphaned of both giver and receiver, a book no one else can understand. The world reduces to things, mute objects whose meaning cannot be expressed except by those who have lived them, and which George turns to now in the search for his mother.

At the end of this passage, Barbara attempts to break George out of this morbid pattern, prompting him to leave, trying to tell him that he is freed as well as orphaned by his mother's death. He is unresponsive, and in the end she is forced to give up by his refusal to speak:

> Barbara: There's nothing to keep you here, you know,
>   George.
> George: No.
> Barbara: It's none of my business.
> George: No.
> Barbara: I'd like Dad's silver cup.

Barbara, above all others, knows George, and leads the dance around him I have already written of, the accommodation of his secrets and problems into the daily life of this world. It is with the tact of an expert negotiator that she shows Doreen, on her return to the cottage, that what she wants is impossible, delicately touching on what she knows about George and what she knows about Doreen without ever needing to say out loud the central fact that makes them incompatible:

> Doreen: How will he manage?
> Barbara: He's quite self-sufficient, Doreen, you know.
> Doreen: Oh yes. But on his own. Will he manage?
> Barbara: Well, he will miss her. She was very fond of him,
>   you see. I never minded. I didn't really.
> Doreen: They got on.
> Barbara: Yes. He's a solitary one. I think he's not someone
>   for you, Doreen.
> Doreen: No.
> Barbara: I don't think he's for marrying, Doreen, you see.
> Doreen: No. I see that. I'll keep an eye on him, though.

Doreen, it seems clear, knows this as well as Barbara does. But it is too late for her, and for me this last line is the saddest line in the whole play – she knows she is not going to be loved by George, but it doesn't matter to her. She is in love, and unable to do anything about it. She must go on. She'll go on.

It is now that time folds back on itself, and we return to the 'present' that began the play, as the envelope closes around this small tragedy and John returns in the clothes he was wearing in the first scene from popping out to the car. John, it is clear, has come to try one more time to shake George out of the life he is living, out here on the moors.

> George: Why did you come then?
> John: You want your pound's worth, don't you?
> George: What do you mean?
> John: Don't.
> George: Well, you said make a break. A clean break.
> John: You can be hard.
> George: Aye. I can be hard. What about you? What are
> you? You're more compassionate, are you? I think you
> are.

This last concession of compassion aside, it is clear George is closed off to the idea of John and the other world he offers. Slowly, John forces him to confront the situation:

> John: Look at you. It's just looking at your... I can't. When
> I see your mouth and your hair. Oh please. Come back
> with me.
> George: Don't talk soft.
> John: I know. I know. Stupid.
> George: If you said jump in the lake, I'd do it. There's not
> much you couldn't make me do.
> John: Except what I want you to do.

Here we encounter the limits of love – or rather, the way love is limited when two people meet across too much distance. The lives George and John lead are too far apart, and George cannot imagine crossing them:

> John: You liked London.
> George: I did. I did. It was all right. It was great for a visit.
> All the visits. But what would I do? Where would I live?
> In your little room, sleeping in that three-quarter bed?

John encourages George to go into acting, but again, George knows he will never belong in that world: 'No. No thanks. Just be some Northerner as a job.' George then forces John to admit that the distance is uncrossable both ways – John couldn't come to York either, as George remorselessly outlines. The play then ends in an awful silence, as Gill presents a closing loveless trio onstage with the entrance of Doreen. Using her as cover, John slips out of the cottage without saying goodbye to George. And the play ends, and Doreen and George are alone on stage together, trapped in their lives.

On some level, then, this is a play about the limits and failures of love, its inability to pull people out of the limits of their lives. But more than this, it seems to me to be a play about belonging, about the way people are walled into their lives regardless of choice, by circumstance and chance, where they are born, who they fall for, and so on. By chance, George, John and Doreen all lose their hearts in this house. They are left with pale imitations of what they want – a grate that should be pulled down but is kept because a lover liked it; friendship, and the right to drop into a house, but not to stay the night there; a peculiar compulsion, on visiting York, to drive out into the middle of nowhere. Small compensations for a life.

★

By the time *Certain Young Men* and *The York Realist* were produced in quick succession at the turn of the millennium, Gill had left the National Theatre as an Associate Director, an ending documented elsewhere in Richard Eyre's diaries, collected as *National Service*. This brought to an end a long phase of Gill's career when he had been associated with and sustained by a building. He had courted such a relationship from the outset through his engagement with the Royal Court, working there as Press Officer, assistant director, actor and eventually writer and director, at first turning up at the end of the week uncertain of whether there would be a paycheck for him, whether the work he had done that week had been on payroll or not. The benefits of these secure relationships had been manifold, but the back-to-back successes of *Certain Young Men* and *The York Realist*, which transferred into the West End, underlined an element of reinvigoration to Gill's work as he went freelance for the first time in a long time. Over the subsequent years he has benefited from a significant number of younger directors entering positions of power in the theatre who, through working with him at the Studio or growing up watching his productions, had developed a relatively awed appreciation for his work and what it stood for, and since leaving the National has been able to work across Britain in a wide variety of institutions whose artistic directors have been proud to support his work and collaborate with him. Prominent among these have been Stephen Unwin, whose advocacy of *The York Realist* as artistic director of English Touring Theatre brought that play to the stage; Michael Grandage, who as artistic director of Sheffield Theatres produced a festival of Gill's work in 2002, a major retrospective for which Gill adapted Wedekind's *Lulu Plays*, writing a play called *Original Sin*, and who went on to engage Gill as a director as well as producing a revival directed by Gill of *Small Change* as artistic director of the Donmar Warehouse; and Josie Rourke, with whom Gill has worked both at the Bush and, again, at the Donmar. He has also directed during the period for the National Theatre and the RSC, and enjoyed a certain amount of commercial success – as well as *The York Realist*, his production of *The Importance of Being Earnest* also transferred into the West End. His writing during this period has included two plays for radio, *The Look Across the Eyes* and *Lovely Evening*, a play for the National Theatre Connections programme called *Friendly Fire*, his memoir *Apprenticeship*, which is interesting as a window on a particular period of theatre history but fascinating as another playful study of memory from Gill, *Certain Young Men*, *The York Realist* and *Original Sin*.

Gill has also maintained his fruitful relationship with Peter Hall, the man who hired him at the National. Working for the Peter Hall Company at Theatre Royal Bath, Gill has directed *Look Back In Anger* and *The Importance of Being Earnest* (a wonderful double bill, it should be noted), and in 2009 directed a new play of his own in Bath's Ustinov Studio. This play, which did not transfer into London and so has not been seen by most of the audience of the majority of Gill's work (the vast majority of Gill's theatre has been produced in London – Grandage's festival was in part motivated out of a desire to bring work to the regions that was not otherwise being seen there, but in general Gill's plays are too often thought not to be suitable for regional revival. I have heard one extraordinary story from an artistic director of a regional theatre who was chastised for producing a play of Gill's that his audience, deemed the powers that be, were unlikely to appreciate due to its complexity). This play, *Another Door Closed*, is a fascinating subject to turn to as this study begins to draw to a close, being as it is a study of mortality, memory and the approach of death.

Writing about an artist whose career is ongoing is a difficult thing to conclude satisfactorily. 'To be continued' is no way to round off an argument, but any attempt to impose a sense of cohesion or completion on the arc of a living writer's work is false. Gill is still writing, and is well capable of producing work in the next few years that turns all I have said here on its head and renders my ideas about his work redundant, as is the case with studies of any living artist. But Gill's work has always been a way of reflecting and interrogating the preoccupations and experiences of his life as he has lived it, and so as he enters his seventies it is perhaps natural that *Another Door Closed* is one of a number of projects in recent years which have seen him working in a retrospective, excavatory mood – not only through directing his first production in Cardiff, of *A Provincial Life*, a play receiving its first production that was also nearly fifty years old in a place Gill has occupied without visiting throughout his work in the theatre, but also through the publication of his time-capsule memoir, *Apprenticeship*. *Another Door Closed*, which featured half of the original company of *Small Change* and returned to the Cardiff of that play and Gill's other early plays for a further meditation on what has happened to that place during the course of Gill's life.

I suspect the writing of *Another Door Closed* was in part prompted while Gill worked at the Donmar on his 2007 revival of *Small Change*. Gill revised the play noticeably for that production – replacing all uses of the word 'toilet' with 'loo' was the change that stuck out most for me when I saw it, presumably a revision of the social squeamishness of Mrs Harte – but also adding a speech about the flowering of tower blocks in Cardiff that very much updated the world of the play in accordance with architectural developments in his home town. This re-writing, it seems to me, may have been part of what stirred his subconscious and preoccupied it once more with the vanished world of his childhood. *Another Door Closed* is the result – another look, thirty-five years after *Small Change*, at the way his home city has been effaced by the passing of time, and at the effacing actions time performs on people and the places they live.

★

Another Door Closed was first presented by the Peter Hall Company at the Theatre Royal Bath, on 4 August 2009. The cast was as follows:

Woman One – June Watson
Woman Two – Marjorie Yates
Man – Sean Chapman

Directed by Peter Gill
Designed by Jessica Curtis
Lighting designer: Paul Pyant
Sound designer: Marcus Christensen
Composer: Christian Mason
Casting director: Amy Ball

★

Woman One: But now we have our own life. We have
    forgotten all that.
Woman Two: It comes back. It comes back.

Another Door Closed is a simple story. Two ageing sisters living together are visited by a man who has sought them out having gone back to the place where they used to live to find their old home has been pulled down. He has not come to visit them, but in the hope of seeing their mother, who has in fact died. The women appear not to know him at first, but then reveal they do remember who he was, and that their Father had taken an inter-est in him after the man's mother had died – in fact, the womens' father helped him get work on a ship, and the man went to sea. The first woman wants to get rid of the man, but the second woman persuades her to let him stay for a drink. The man stays, has a beer with them, tries to give them the present he had brought for their mother, but causes an argument and leaves. His presence prompts reflection and discussion between the three characters about the past they share – how they felt about the deceased mother and the deceased father of the family, how they feel about their vanished, younger lives.

The play grows out of simple components. The opening stage directions recall later Beckett in their precision and simplicity:

> *Woman One, inside the closed front door, facing front holding two shopping bags.*
> *Woman Two, sitting facing the open back door.*

This is not quite Footfalls, however, as Gill also begins the play by noting: 'the layout of the dialogue is not intended to be prescriptive. It does not indicate a system of pauses or silences, but is there to make for easier reading and to give some general indication of rhythm and flow.' Gill's insistence on the written text as only the surface of the play, not a place for careful conducting, which is done in the rehearsal room, reminds us that he comes from a Royal Court school of directors whose insis-tence on the playscript as a document to be used to generate a performance, not to be read in a living room, was at the centre of their reading of the theatre as a primarily practical trade.

The play's initial exchanges also have a Beckettian quality, as, like a musical or mathematical structure, they steadily grow through repetition and variation of simple elements. The opening exchange seems almost like a children's game:

> Woman One: Are you in? Are you there, dear?

> Woman Two: Yes, dear. I'm here dear. Are you in?
> Woman One:
> Are you?
> Are you in? Oo-oo. Are you there?

This repetitive sequence – which is at one level two women not hearing each other properly, but is so densely patterned and heavily repetitious as to abstract that scene, making it something larger, a wider mis-hearing or not-hearing between the two characters – is succeeded, wavelike, by another dialogue that develops through accrual and variation:

> Woman Two: I'm here with you in this lovely light, throw-
> ing bread crumbs through the back door for the birds.
> Woman One: Are you?
> Woman Two: I'm hearing throwing breadcrumbs through
> the back door for the birds.
> Woman One: Through the window for the birds.
> Woman Two: Through the back door for the birds.

There is also a touch of the long-suffering, passive-aggressive co-habiting relationship in that last correction, a line to bring a smile to the lips of the audience that establishes an interesting undercurrent to this primarily unsettling play – it is regularly quite funny, because of what the two women say to each other.

What we are seeing in these opening exchanges is a rhythm indicative of the larger life of these characters: exchanges imbued with such regularity and simplicity as to seem emblematic of multiple exchanges, that are only interrupted and provoked into any more meaningful speech by the intrusion of the Man into the house, who arrives with a Pinteresque 'hello' to end a scene shortly after Woman One has returned with the shopping.

The play then proceeds to detail the disappointment of a visitor who has thought he would find one thing but finds another, and the discomfort of two women forced to rake up their past. These feelings coalesce round the deceased mother of the two women, who is invoked as a potent absence in the house even before the Man's arrival. Woman One daydreams about where her mother could have got to at length, in another passage structured around repetition and variation, wondering aloud, 'is she in the garden, is she? Is she pulling up the line? Are the sheets high in the wind, is she looking up at the sheets high up against the sky?' She goes on to ask other questions – 'is she cutting back the lilac, is she?', or 'is she on the landing, looking out, looking through the window is she?' – before the scope of her questioning expands and she asks of the house in general and of her sister as well, 'is there spring in the sofa, salt in the jar, suet in the pudding, the dripping on the toast, the wood in the hole, the fat in the fire, the nigger in the woodpile? Are there enough darning needles? Is there buckram and butter muslin?' The function of this speech is twofold: it is at one level a woman asking, is all right with the world?, and simultaneously creating her own echoing 'no' for an answer – what she dreams of as an ordered and well balanced life is a collection of long vanished cultural indicators, as evocative of a sense of time and place as the lists David Kynaston weaves into his *Tales of a New Jerusalem*, speaking of different worlds, attitudes, habits and lives that are undoubtedly vanished from the world of these old women, who still are in recovery from their childhood, reverting to the ideas of their childhood as their image of what is right and normal, still thinking of their childhood as their real lives.

The Man finds these changes just as difficult to accept:

> Man: Strange for me, this. It's hard to take in.
> I took it for granted that you would be there still.
> Why wouldn't you be?
> Not prepared, not prepared at all, you know, for it to
> all be gone like that...
> It's gone, it's gone, you know, your home. Well, of
> course, you must know. It's all gone all down there.
> All of it.

He, too, is confronted by a disappeared world, one that he has held sacred and wanted to find intact on his return: 'it's always fear amid fantasy when you are away for so long and so far, but it's a comfort, it's your loneliness, to dream of someone constant, in your exile. The thought of her always bright in my mind then, for I was away for so long, you see.' Thinking of the dead mother he wanted to see, he tells her daughters that she 'called me her little soldier. And it's gone, the haven of my childhood.' He cannot believe what has happened to them either: 'you were little girls with ribbons and white dresses at first and then young ladies in waisted costumes and hats and gloves.'

This amazement and disbelief, the central event of the play, the disillusionment of the Man, is then interestingly confronted by Gill through the responses of the two women. The women flatten his sense of shock, insisting that he may find it extraordinary, but that it's also perfectly normal:

> Woman Two: He remembers us as little girls with ribbons.
> Woman One: We were little girls with ribbons, dear.

The womens' response seems almost to become a rebuke to Gill's years of revisiting the Cardiff of his past, as they reject the Man's expectation that they might have stayed preserved in aspic for the pleasure his own memories might provide him. It is the Man who first acknowledges that they have moved on from the girls he knew:

> Man: You have moved on and now it is as if your feminin-
>   ity was something not worth holding on to.

Woman One refuses to let this be spoken of with such a sense of pathetic decline as he offers with that line, however.

> Woman One: We have moved on you see. You want us to
>   remain where we were to suit you.

Woman One, who takes a dislike to the Man where Woman Two is more welcoming, detects low motives and refuses to be boxed into a simple meaning for his purposes:

> Woman One: He expects to find that we are disappointed
>   women, isn't that it? And to pick at the shame of our

being so, to see us pick at the scab of our shame... Our
life looks a poor thing, is that what he thinks?

She also refuses to accept his memory of the time when they
knew each other as the truth, laying her own contradictory
memories over his impressions like tracing paper over a map:

> Woman One: I only can recall unease and fear and not
> knowing, that went with the vivacity he wants to recall.

The impression persists that much of what Woman One says
is in some way reflecting on Gill, and his persistent attention to
the world she inhabits. However, in assaulting his returns home
in fiction, she also embodies much that Gill's work has always
been trying to say: that people such as her are insistently and
gloriously alive, more complex than anyone can successfully
depict, and likely to slip out from under you if you try to pin
them down. Woman One's rebuttal of the Man's attempt to lock
them into the status of memories, not living people, climaxes with
a neat insult:

> Woman One: He is like a cuckoo, he has returned to find
> an empty nest.

Martin Amis has written that once a writer is born into a
family, that family is dead. And perhaps Gill's family has always
been the Cardiff of his childhood, and he could indeed be envis-
aged as a cuckoo, drawing on the lives and tales of others to
develop his own imaginative world: perhaps that is the rebuttal
Gill offers himself in this play. But he has never drawn on these
stories for his own nourishment or advancement. He has always
done so to prove precisely the second point: that the people he
writes about are alive, and free, and will fly the nest when he isn't
looking. That the world is larger and more alive than the London
theatre audience had previously imagined it.

In the context of Gill's previous work, *Another Door Closed*
brings a strong sense of cohesion to some of what Gill has been
doing throughout his writing career. I have written of *Mean Tears*

that the play examined a Catholic sense of exile; I have detailed Gill's own idea that to go into the theatre is to exile oneself from one's own class; and I have invoked the ghost of James Joyce, who tried to put all of Dublin into a book while living far away from that city in a self-imposed exile. And throughout this book I have read Gill's plays as a study of distance – of the distances between people imposed by time, geography, experience, by our very skin, by what I fear we must call 'the human condition', which is so beautifully analysed in *Certain Young Men*, the possibility of ever crossing that distance and making a genuine, meaningful contact with another human being, and the longing that exists as a result of distance, absence, space. Gill has always written about exile, about love across distances, about the isolation experienced by us all as a basic component of what it means to be alive. Throughout his writing, he has returned to his experience and idea of isolation and distance, interrogated how it develops with time, phrased and rephrased his philosophy with different plays to offer different subplots to the larger story he has to tell about being alone in life, at sea in an open boat, tossed by the waves. *Another Door Closed* allowed me to see Gill's work as somewhat akin to Proust's *a la recherché du temps perdu* – a sequence of individual works that collectively build to phrase a larger idea about human experience, more potent and profound when viewed as a whole, the beads on the rosary of his bibliography giving voice collectively to the prayer that lies behind them and prompts their iteration in the first place. *Another Door Closed*, in the context of *The Sleepers Den, Over Gardens Out, Small Change* and *Cardiff East*, is an inevitable play – a further address of Gill's long, loving look back into his past. John Burgess argued that the silence between *Over Gardens Out* and *Small Change* was necessary while Gill formulated a new statement; these periodic silences and utterances have always been necessary, as Gill has waited for the ground under his feet to shift sufficiently for the view of life afforded him to change and offer new insight that can become the material for a play.

The new development in *Another Door Closed* is the stark intrusion into the story of a quite different kind of death to

anything we have read or seen in Gill before. Death in Gill is a
regular event, but in other plays it is the mother who dies – Old
Mrs Shannon, Mrs Harte, Mrs Driscoll's deaths are the subjects
of those plays but those stories are told from the perspective of a
younger generation. In *Another Door Closed*, that generation for
the first time confronts the certainty of death approaching them.
This gives a new focus and solidity to a staple of Gill's work, the
attempt to grapple with the existential by his characters. Where
Mrs Shannon tried and failed to express frustration, Gerard tries
and fails to put his finger on the moment when he became
himself, Woman Two confronts us with a far more concrete
thought.

> Woman Two: Will there be pain?
> Woman One: Close it now, dear.
> Woman Two: Will there be time, dear?
> Woman One: I expect so, dear.
> Woman Two: Will I have time?
> Woman One: Time, dear, for what?
> Woman Two: To finish my work.

This last line gives the suggestion that we are hearing Gill's
thoughts as much as the woman's, and the fact that this play was
produced in his seventieth year bears down on the line, which
becomes an insistent question one must, perhaps, begin to ask
seriously when one reaches seventy. This unprecedented stare at
death is accompanied by a new fatalism, a new defeatism, evoked
by the Man. This play, it strikes me, asks harder questions than
its predecessors. It is easy enough for a writer in the brightness
of their life to ask questions about what being alive is like, to draw
attention to the numinous qualities of the everyday and work to
restore and burnish the dignity and beauty of apparently
unremarkable lives. But when that same writer is, in Clive James's
phrase, 'approaching his terminus', and confronting in art the
fact that dignity and beauty aside, the limits being staged are
whole lives and, when those lives end, will have constituted the
whole lives of people, it is understandable that a new anger and
darkness might come into the voice. The Man grapples with the

past's refusal to stoke any kind of warm glow, with the subjectivity of his remembered experience. When he asks, 'doesn't it mean what it means to me?', he is struggling with the refusal of memory to become beautiful and numinous in the minds of his conversant – with the fact that the hallucinogenic qualities Gill has always imbued in ordinary life can also abandon those lives and leave them forgettable. He tells Woman Two when her sister goes to look for a beer, 'reality has hit me hard in the face. It can be such a lacklustre thing, can't it?' This is an inversion of the Lawrentian trope Gill has explored throughout his work. It confronts the drabness and ordinariness of life as it begins to draw itself up, to tie off its ends, a vision of the world we have not seen from Gill before.

In that context, it is interesting to puzzle over the title of this play. What is the meaning of this phrase, 'another door closed'? It offers, for me, a melancholy reading of the action a play performs on the psyche of its writer. Like Amis's family, a play in this reading seems to kill off the life it captures, as Aboriginals believe a photograph steals a soul. Here is a poignant reading of a writing career: that each time Gill gathered together the material with which to make his new statements, what he was also doing was closing chapters of his life, completing a certain train of thought, signing off spheres of experience as he moved through his life, trying to hold onto things as he went but able only in the final equation to gather together experiences as markers left behind him for other people to pick up, read, perhaps revive one day in a form of creative excavation. The artist Andy Goldsworthy makes work not unlike this. He goes out into wildernesses, collects natural elements there – stones, driftwood – and arranges them into simple patterns before photographing them and leaving. The photograph, like a first night review, records the event – and the sculpture itself, presumably, is left in the middle of nowhere, surviving for a little while, perhaps for no time at all if it is just a parting made through grass, fragments shored against the ruins of the artist's life that it might just be possible for another wanderer to find. In this reading of a play, an opening night is also a closing off of creative possibility, as all the nebulous

material of a subconscious takes a definite and single form and in
so doing excludes the infinite possible other forms it might have
taken. In this reading, the end of each day when the back door of
the sisters' house is closed and the second woman stops feeding
the birds is another day gone and vanished from their lives and
their future, leaving the sisters shorter of breath and one day
closer to death. The questions, which once were spoken by
existentially concerned young men trying to realise themselves,
keep getting harder and more brutal as they are now put into the
voices of old women:

> Dear?
> Will there be pain?
> Dear?
> Will there be time?

And still Gill's voices cry out across a distance, seeking
someone else who will call back an answer, seeking to make a
connection between one human being and another.

★

Versailles was first performed at the Donmar Warehouse on
February 20th, 2014.

Edith Rawlinson – Francesca Annis
Constance – Helen Bradbury
Marjorie Chater – Barbara Flynn
Arthur Chater – Christopher Godwin
Angela Isham – Selina Griffiths
Gerald Chater – Tom Hughes
Mabel – Tamla Kari
Henry Sedgwick Bell – Edward Killingback
Leonard – Gwilym Lee
Geoffrey Ainsworth – Adrian Lukis
Hugh Skidmore – Josh O'Connor
The Hon. Frederick Gibb – Simon Williams
Ethel – Eleanor Yates

Directed by Peter Gill
Designed by Richard Hudson
Lighting Designer: Paul Pyant
Sound Designer: Gregory Clarke

★

There will be time enough, it transpires, for a fair bit more to be said. When I began writing this book, which grew out of many conversations with Gill about the theatre we believed in, the theatre we saw around us now, and the theatre we wanted to make, he informed me that he was in the early stages of writing a new play. I was fortunate to have opportunities to read this project as it developed, reading the first two acts in draft form at his flat one afternoon and encountering a story of the Versailles conference, of the home life and work life of a young man working on aspects of the Versailles treaty relating to coal production. I rather simplistically categorised it to myself as a play to follow *The York Realist*, a study of a social world (this time the world of upper middle class Kent and the Hotel Astoria in Paris during the negotiations), which engaged me as a reader because the play's strongest argument seemed to be the common humanity between myself and the people making these decisions. But there is also something new about this play, an element I did not think Gill had written before. His plays, for me, had always been voices from the wilderness, outsider stories; in this story, in the lead-up to the centenary of the Great War, he had put his finger on the moment when the course of the entire twentieth century was decided, and chosen to dramatise it. *Versailles*, as the play was called, was an exposition on who we are as a culture, as a world even, and why that is so. By looking at a moment when western culture questioned its structures and its future, he found a way to analyse the values and structures which were reinforced or put in place as a result of the Versailles treaty, and furthermore the values and structures which underpinned the decision-making process that made that treaty what it was. It was the most eloquent and explicit political statement of Gill's I had read, and I hoped fervently that it would find a producer, not only because of the play's qualities, but selfishly because I saw before me a far more satisfying possible conclusion to the narrative arc of this study than was presently available to me.

Gill is not a prolific writer, and I met him and got to know his work during one of the long interludes between plays which have characterised his career: by the time I began writing this book, he had not had a new play in London for over a decade. I didn't think this made a particular difference to what I wanted to write, but I confess it concerned me that the last play I would address in detail during my study was *Another Door Closed*, a play which is haunting, mesmeric, beautiful and deeply concerned with ideas of mortality and decline. I hardly felt I would be doing Gill any favours if I ended on that note. So I was delighted when I learned during the interviews for this book that Josie Rourke was to produce *Versailles* for the Donmar. Rourke, whose career began as an assistant at the Donmar, where she worked with Gill before going on to work with him again around the country before running the Bush and then returning to the Donmar as its artistic director, credits Gill as one of the governing influences on her work, and makes theatre I love for the way it draws on Gill's own ideas, and the Donmar is the perfect home for Gill's new play. So I am now able to end this book, not in Bath in 2009 with a play about people fading away, but in the heart of Covent Garden, on the very night of this book's publication, which has been cannily timed to appear during the run of *Versailles*. It is a tremendous pleasure for me to be publishing this book as Gill's new play reiterates his clear-sighted intelligence, his importance as a writer, his value to the theatre. I cannot know, of course, how the play has gone down – this manuscript went to the printers long before *Versailles* went into rehearsal or the critics sharpened their pencils and found their seats in the stalls – but by way of augury I am put in mind of a conversation I had with Gill walking round Shepherd's Bush in 2010, while we prepared for the press night of *The Aliens*. Full of youthful enthusiasm, I asked Gill whether he was looking forward to the evening. 'Oh, no,' he replied. 'They'll either say "oh, the Great Gill", or they'll be respectfully dismissive, but no one will actually review it.' Having fallen headlong into the former camp myself, I look forward to discovering how accurate an analysis of this latest bout of critical opinion this summation proves to be.

In order to comment on *Versailles*, I have borrowed a copy of the play's rehearsal draft, and will quote from this in the course of my reading. This draft may, of course, differ here and there from the script as performed at the Donmar, or as published by Faber and Faber – but I trust it will not alter so materially as to make criticism meaningless, and I must beg the indulgence of the reader and hope the interest of engaging critically with a play before it has even reached the stage compensates for any redundancies which may creep in. If anyone happens to be reading this passage before they go to see the production, I would advise you, in time-honoured Match of the Day style, to look away now...

Versailles is a ghost story about loves stopped by the Great War. The play begins in a house in Kent, where Edith, playing patience, complains to her daughter Mabel that her son Hugh has not yet returned from the war:

> Edith: How long before he's home for good?
> Mabel: I don't know.
> Edith: Why is it taking so long?
> Mabel: Well I suppose they can't disperse a whole army in a trice.
> Edith: There are other boys home now. Ethel's brother, William, is here. Why isn't Hugh?
> Mabel: It's not Hugh's fault, Mummy. You sound as if he could do something about it.
> Edith: No, poor boy, I know. But why should it be so for some and different for others?
> Mabel: Ours not mother.

Plot devices are established by the conversation of the two women before anyone else enters the stage, notably a putative marriage to an unnamed individual which is clearly the cause of some discomfort between mother and daughter:

> Edith: And then?

Mabel: What then?

Edith: Well, dear.

Mabel: Well, dear, what, mother?

Edith: Haven't you spoken?

Mabel: Mummy, not now, not now.

Edith: You won't be able to put things off for ever, you
know. It won't be fair.

It is established that Mabel has brought a guest to the house
from London on the same day Edith has invited the Chaters, a
couple from the village whose son was killed in the war, to tea. It
is also established that the play takes place in an atmosphere of
unsettling normality, where the characters are afflicted by a sense
that life is moving inexorably on from the tragedy of the previous
years, about which Edith is particularly eloquent:

Edith: Things have become so ordinary and everyday
again in such a short time... instead of being, as we
were, united in one preoccupation, we are all leading
our separate lives again and going our separate ways.

This, it is clear, is to be an aftermath play, a study of the ashes
of the war, after the idealism and collectivism and hope of the
period have evaporated. Edith dislikes this new, post-war world
intensely, and is aware that for people like the Chaters, it means
being left behind:

Edith: When I went into Tonbridge on Wednesday, the
sameness was oppressing. As if nothing had happened
at all. There was no difference in the shops, except that
when I went for tea in Brewsters, there seemed to be a
greater variety of sugar cakes and currant buns on
offer. But no soldiers anywhere. And now having to
deal with what is ahead. Whatever that is. Except for
those like the poor Chaters, who are left isolated in
their grief, increasingly to become, I suppose, more
lonely and cut off.

The world, Edith knows, is not the one the Chaters knew any

more, and is seeking to 'go forward again'. There have been alter-
ations in the lives of Edith and Mabel as well, changes reflected
in a diminution of staff in the house:

> Edith: Oh, let's not wait for the Chaters. Mabel, go and
> ask if we can have tea.
> Mabel: Why can't we ring for Ethel?
> Edith: There is only the two of them now, Mabel, and
> dinner to get.

Shorn of staff and surrounded by new attitudes, these women
face an altered reality. Edith and Mabel are joined on stage by the
other house guests, and by Leonard, Edith's other son, who is
looking for an old atlas:

> Geoffrey: And why an old atlas, may I ask?
> Leonard: I've only brought maps that are current, like an
> idiot, and I find I need reference before eighteen
> seventy.
> Geoffrey: Not only carrying the bags then.
> Leonard: It's thought I know something about coal
> production.
> Geoffrey: And do you?
> Leonard: I'm beginning to know more than I did.

This is a delightful sketch of the amateurism of a particular
class, the men who have been tasked with dividing up Europe
and thereby deciding its political future. Geoffrey, Leonard and
the assembled party go on to discuss David Lloyd-George's
plans for the Germans, and the views to be heard at Geoffrey's
club:

> Geoffrey: Oh, I've lost completely any of the admiration I
> had for the Germans before the war... I am afraid that
> all I admired there was no more than a mask over
> something baser than we ever dreamt of... And I may
> say you know my views are relatively quiet, compared
> to those you would hear expressed in my club.

The group are then joined by Mrs Chater, whose grief-stricken husband has excused himself, unable to get through an afternoon in company following his son's death, and the grieving Mrs Chater offers an initially simpler, clearer, more forceful and moral position on her hopes for the Versailles treaty:

> Mrs Chater: Peace, peace at all costs. Who could wish
> otherwise? But I imagine there is a bill to pay for this
> war and who is to pay for it pray? Should we who
> didn't seek it?

As she expands on her position, however, the moral high ground granted her as a result of the loss she has suffered begins to slip away:

> Mrs Chater: As things stand, I feel we are being overcome
> by all kinds of ideas that are alien to us, many of them
> foreign in origin and which are superseding that which
> is natural in us. I feel it as an English woman... I feel
> our values are being gradually eroded by influences
> outside us... I am behind in all things I know. Would
> you let her marry a nigger then? You see what a shock
> plain speaking produces.

Mrs Chater's language shocks us out of the easy, civil vernacular of the play's discourse, a sharp underlining of the powerful and violent ideas being batted idly round this room. In doing so, she also sketches out two positions: that of the objectionable reactionary, but also that of the mass of men and women, giving perhaps a more coarsely honest voice to the sense of being left behind that Edith earlier suspected in her. Mrs Chater emerges as a symbol of ossified, irrelevant and outdated England, a world which feels itself overtaken by circumstances. She is a rock around which the tide is ebbing throughout the play. Geoffrey, hedging diplomatically, aligns himself with the essential feeling of her speech, her impression of being outflanked: 'I think we are in danger of taking on more than we can digest in every way.' His own conservative views are then challenged by the younger, more liberal, more progressive and bohemian characters on the stage, Mabel and her friend Constance:

> Mabel: You are not a democrat then, Geoffrey.
> Edith: Democrat is such an un-English word.
> Geoffrey: A limited democracy of course. The people must have a voice.
> Mabel: Who selects the elite?
> Geoffrey: Oh, they emerge. As it happens now. Look at Leonard.
> Constance: Are they all male?

This, as Edith's contribution points out, is a classic intergenerational clash; the new world of the young pushing forwards, the elders holding on to what was there before. We see a social system in operation, two patterns clashing (progressive v conservative), a contest which is in itself the revealed workings of a third established social machine (young v old). As Mabel says of the walk the group have been on that afternoon, 'people usually say it's so English. Which indeed it is.'

What *Versailles* then goes on to do is to ask whether those machines could not be redesigned. The Versailles conference is here dramatised as the twentieth century's great missed opportunity, and, to a point, its great tragedy – the moment, more than any other single point in the last century, when the world could have been remodelled to work more humanely, and the moment when almost every tragedy of the subsequent hundred years was set in motion by the passing up of that opportunity. Gill's perspective on the event, writing almost a century later, is an important aspect of the play, as hindsight allows him to forecast consequences for the treaty, which is read in this play, not as the end of a war, but as the start of something far greater, a whole world of events and changes and continuities.

What is felt by all the assembled party in Gill's first act is that they are living in a moment of great change, when the world is taking a new shape around them. As Constance sees it, 'we have reached a tipping point or perhaps the tipping point has been already reached and we still have the outcome to face.' These discussions prove inconclusive, leading nowhere but round and round the stage, as the play's first act is characterised by anticipation. It is only once the tea party breaks up and Leonard is left alone on stage, having been told by Mrs Chater that she has found some letters to her dead son Gerald from before the war, that the drama's emotional heart is revealed, as the ghost of Gerald appears to Leonard:

> Gerald: What do I say?
> Leonard: Hello.
> Gerald: Mm?
> Leonard: Nothing your mother couldn't read.
> Gerald: No.
> Leonard: Except...
> Gerald: Miss you...
> Leonard: Yes.
> Gerald: Love...

Leonard is hiding a private grief from his family and from Mrs Chater, which he will perhaps never be able to reveal: that he has been robbed of the person he felt closest to, and still imagines him near at hand, unable to lay the thought of Gerald to rest. Sudden and violent death has no narrative order to it. Relationships are not allowed to run a full course and end as satisfyingly as a story does, as they are when two people drift apart within the course of their lives; a sense to the loved person's ending cannot be superimposed through recourse to the nature of their illness to explain what is happening. Sudden and violent death is a robbery, and leaves every phrase of the life that has ended incomplete and suspended cruelly in the air. For those, like Mrs Chater or Leonard, who were involved in that life, it is like a part of them has been abruptly amputated. These visitations from Gerald, which run through *Versailles*, resemble phantom limb syndrome, the amputee's experience of still feeling the part of themselves they have lost as if it were attached to their body. They are Gill's way of expressing the ongoing inner life of Leonard, who imagines Gerald into being whenever he is alone. Gerald returns at the beginning of Act Two, which is set in the

Hotel Astoria in Paris, where Leonard is trying, at the eleventh hour, to change some details of the proposed redistribution of the Silesian coal fields.

> Gerald: Finding it hard.
> Leonard: Proving so. Yes.
> Gerald: Not expected.
> Leonard: Not really no. Not like this at any case.
> Gerald: Politics.
> Leonard: The politics of politics.

Gerald is Leonard's imaginary conscience, his dream confessor (and in Peter Gill's work, that word should never be invoked lightly – but it is surely the case that Gerald is an aspect of the confessional in Gill's subconscious), allowing him to engage with all his uncertainty and anger through imagined dialogue. Gerald himself seeks to understand the role he is playing in Leonard's subconscious as the second act proceeds:

> Gerald: This is a might have been is it? Now, things are other between us. To be put aside, at a distance, accessed to order. For you to mull over at leisure, like a novelist might, preparing an account of all this on his own terms. Skewing it his way, without the inconvenience of including my thinking, perhaps, that nothing might have happened. Or what I think might have happened. So this I tucked away, as a might have been romance.

Gill furnishes Gerald with a detached, intelligent perspective on events around Leonard, which allows a noticeably modern understanding of what is happening at the Astoria to be expressed on stage. There is perhaps some risk in this device, allowing Gerald to speak with all the understanding which a century of subsequent history has given Gill, to foretell change and contextualise event through his eloquent reading of Leonard's problems. I always find it rather pathetic whenever I watch a BBC costume drama set in the nineteenth century where the hero is obviously a *Guardian* reader whose liberal, libertarian views of life precisely coincide with the most earnestly left-leaning sensibilities of the percentile of that costume drama's audience that lives in Crouch End (where the commissioning editor for the second series invariably lives). But the past can indisputably be used as a way of passing comment on the present, and it is in the contextualisation offered by Gerald that *Versailles* finds its contemporary relevance and becomes more than a regressive period curiosity, an episode of *Downton Abbey* on stage. Gerald insists in the first act that the Great War must surely have necessitated a redrawing of the social and political machinery of the world:

> Gerald: Much of what I aspired to was a pose, free as it was, a fake. For us, for any one of the middling class, to go on taking part in the same way as we did before this, would be a betrayal, you know. We, who have been educated to act as the managers of the system that created this. Those of us destined to lead a troop, to run a department, to advise a Cabinet minister, to manage investment, to publish a book, to run a district, educated to make things more efficient, to ameliorate the worst, the better to keep it going. We, on the second rung, we, who are trained for the service of this... we must lend a hand to another enterprise now, or else will be damned.

Gerald's postmodern perspective lies not in any narrative device affecting the play, any insight into future events or any special knowledge about what is going to happen to the rest of the twentieth century, but in Gill gifting him with intelligence and eloquence, and a clear-sightedness which risks sounding like the reflective voice of the playwright speaking within the drama. What excuses this near-intervention from Gill is, firstly, that such views were undoubtedly being discussed and debated during this period in the highly cultured and intelligent circles where the play is set, and also that *Versailles* affects us precisely because it attempts to connect the modern perspective with the historical event. Gerald's intelligence acts as a bridge between the story and the audience – in true Lacanian fashion, because a character on stage reflects deeply on events, further reflection is prompted and encouraged in the audience, as the play becomes emblematic of so many more missed opportunities for change which we can superimpose on the drama. This commentary on the war works very well as a reflection on the 2008 financial crisis, for example, and I would argue for *Versailles* as the most intelligent reflection yet on the way lessons have not been learned in this last decade from the implosion of the systems by which we operate our own lives. Just as theatre laid bare the essence of the problem leading to the 2008 crash in Lucy Prebble's *ENRON*, here it analyses fruitfully and suggestively the way that nothing has been solved in that crash's aftermath – and by setting that inactivity against the ideological inactivity which followed the Great War, theatre points a way towards the likely event of another collapse of our financial system in the future.

The precise role Gerald plays within Leonard's mind comes in for some questioning, as Gill engages through this construct with one of his abiding themes, the nature of memory:

> Gerald: Some things are present. As this is for you. As things have been for me.
> Leonard: What?
> Gerald: Do you remember your first day at school?
> Leonard: What?
> Gerald: Why do we remember, what we remember?
> Leonard: Oh.
> Gerald: Is it random, memory, neurological, like a dream. Or is it access to what was once so present do you think?... But also randomly, things that seem not important were they?

To question the nature of memory, and why things are important, and which things last in a life, is to question the nature of life, and so for Gerald this is a rich, multilayered passage. He tries to puzzle a meaning to his own life that has ended, as well as to his life as a constructed memory of Leonard's. Gerald's presence on the stage seems to suggest that for Leonard, memory is the second of these options, a route back into what was once present for him, a place where you can 'feel safe in the present moment' of the past, as Gill wrote in *Small Change*.

As well as acting as an extension of Leonard's subconscious, Gerald also performs the useful dramatic function of allowing Leonard an interlocutor with whom he can discuss the issues which press most heavily upon him, giving him an excuse to speak out loud when he is alone and considering the implications of what he is doing. Gill is invaluable as a formal innovator when it comes to finding ways of expressing the interior life of a character on stage. Shakespeare used soliloquies, and Gill's plays are filled with monologue poems, the asides of *Certain Young Men*, the redraftings of *In The Blue*, the juxtaposition of *The York Realist*, the televisions framing *Over Gardens Out*, but here the interior of the character is expressed through providing him with someone to speak to, allowing Leonard room for reflection:

> Leonard: It feels that we may be negotiating a truce rather
> than settling a peace... And then outside it, eddying out
> of Paris across the world, with ever, it seems to me,
> decreasing understanding of things, decisions that
> make what I'm struggling to impress on them now feel
> very small beer.

Leonard carries the concerns of his family home in Kent into the negotiations. The same concerns about the consequences and missed opportunities of this peace which were raised in Kent preoccupy him in the Astoria, as he expresses in conversation with Henry Gibb, one of his superiors on the treaty negotiations who visits his office before attempting to intercede on his behalf with regards to the contested arrangement over Silesia. Leonard explains to him that it will not be possible for coal to be manufactured at the same rate as it was before the war:

> Leonard: I'm sorry but really you know, I think we have
> already forgotten it is all the abstractions and all the
> politics, the effects of war. Man power depleted by the

war. The poor physical condition of the men because of
privation suffered and increasingly the condition of the
collieries. The lack of investment. It is illusory to think
that in the event Germany will be able to pay repara-
tion to the extent proposed and the leaders who tell
their people otherwise will not be telling the truth.

Leonard's most meaningful conversations are with Gerald,
though, when his colleagues leave the stage. Here, the play of
ideas can flow more freely, as Gerald leads Leonard from his
initial, instinctive views to a more fully thought-out position, as
when he suggests of the ideologically compromised negotiations
that 'the task ahead lies in finding an elite whose object is to make
itself redundant.' His implication, of course, is that no such elite
will ever be found. Leonard, less clear of the implications of what
he is doing and led in his opinions by Gerald, questions his views
of what the treaty will accomplish:

> Leonard: Don't you think it will change now. Already
> changing. The world as it was.
> Gerald: No, it will adapt. There will be enough in the
> world to distract the people. Look no further than the
> king, if you want an example of survival. Speak less
> German, abandon your European family, change your
> name and disown your cousin the Kaiser, abandon
> your cousin the Tsar.

Gerald's detached, fatalistic view of the treaty's potential is
driven home to Leonard, as his own approach to the treaty is
questioned and challenged:

> Gerald: When you say France must do this or Germany
> must pay that what do you mean?
> Leonard: What I say.
> Gerald: There is no flesh. The implications, other than
> your own, are rather left out.

The effect of all this is to harden Leonard's views on his work and the work of the entire British delegation at the negotiations, to calcify his ideas of the negotiations as a series of compromises and missed opportunities, to clarify his sense of moral outrage at the work being done to the point where he can barely stomach what is happening around him, as he reveals to his colleague Henry Bell:

> Leonard: How can you be so sanguine?
> Henry Bell: What?
> Leonard: All that is done and dusted is it then your other
>   work? And on to the Middle East.
> Henry: It is.
> Leonard:...Have you cast off the other stuff so easily?
> Henry: Not easily, but yes.

What Leonard begins to see around him is nothing short of a stitch-up: 'surely it's one team of the elect serving another.' Henry Bell, not particularly opposing this view but more easily able to reconcile himself to what is happening, expands on the sense of political 'fudge' things have taken on: 'the farther we get from Paris, the less firm the ground is. Like rowing a boat with a spoon... By the time we get to the Far East, we'll be exhausted.' This prediction seems borne out by Henry Gibb when he returns to Leonard's office to inform him that he has been unable to have any influence on the negotiation over Silesia: 'there's no appetite over there to reconsider any decision already taken, no matter how passionate and rational the advocacy is.' Leonard's participation in the act ends with a visit from Hugh, who tells him that adjustment continues to be difficult for the family at home in Kent, saying of Mabel, 'I think this armistice has left her. I don't know. Perhaps all of us. Uncertain perhaps. Finding adjustment difficult.' Leonard then goes out, leaving Henry Gibb and Leonard's secretary Miss Isham on stage, discussing the state of the treaty. Gill allows himself some sharply ironic lines here, as he sets the expectations of his characters against the events they cannot know will follow from their actions:

> Gibb: The promises we've made to the Arabs and the Jews

in Palestine will need some handling, I think.
Isham: Well, we can do that. The Jews aren't very numerous, are they?

The treaty, again, is envisioned as a great cloud gathering
during the play which, Gill reminds us, will still hang over the
heads of his audience when they walk out of the theatre and try
to find a taxi at the end of the evening.

The third act of the play returns us to Kent, and focuses our
attention finally, not on the Silesian coalfields, but on the intimate
and human problems thrown up by the war which take place in
this house. Constance and Mabel are discussing plans for a war
memorial in the village, and their concerns over how Hugh feels
about this. Their conversation leads on to men needing wives –
Geoffrey in particular they believe – and Edith then enters and
develops this theme, returning us to one of the issues raised in
Act One when she tells Mabel: 'you can't go on leaving Hugh not
knowing where he stands, like this. You can't.' Mabel seems set
against the idea of marriage, and the suggestion of her alignment
to the female suffrage movement enters her argument with Edith:

Edith: Oh stuff. And I don't see that to be graceless and
awkward is the answer.
Mabel: Perhaps a period of gracelessness is necessary for
women.

The Chaters then arrive again for tea, but the gathering is
disrupted when Hugh refuses to look at the plans for the new war
memorial. Mabel then tells him that she cannot marry him, and
Hugh leaves abruptly to visit a friend of his who is recovering
from shell shock in a nearby hospital, telling the assembled party:
'I find it necessary to be with a man who has heard a shell
explode,' and accusing Mabel of forgetting what has happened:
'You've moved on... comparatively.' The act then breaks into a
second scene, which begins with a carefully poised, Chekhovian
conversation between Constance and Geoffrey, who skirt round
the issue of their attraction to each other more or less successfully:

> Geoffrey: I enjoy our meetings. Your company. That's
> rather clumsy of me, but I do.

Leonard then returns to the stage, and is followed closely by
Gerald, who presses the issue of the relationship they might have
had:

> Gerald: If I had come on strong, you would have taken
> flight.
> Leonard: And we'll never know.
> Gerald: No.
> Leonard: Never, never know. I'll never know. This fucking
> war, this fucking, fucking war. I'll never, never, never
> know. It goes round and round, never to know, never.
> Please don't be dead.

Gerald tries to ease Leonard's anger, but only succeeds in
upsetting him further with the remorseless line of argument he
chooses:

> Gerald: You'll forget.
> Leonard: I won't.
> Gerald: You've got this life to lead.
> Leonard: I won't.
> Gerald: You will. Things will take over, they will. You'll
> have to.

The rest of the family then come into the room to join
Leonard, and we learn that he is back in England because he has
resigned from his work at the treaty negotiations:

> Leonard: I found I could no longer do my work.
> Geoffrey: Why?
> Leonard: Oh.
> Edith: Oh, dear.
> Leonard: Confusion, anger, conscience, anger, disillusion,
> conscience. So much that I couldn't work.
> Mrs Chater: Over work do you think perhaps Geoffrey?

> Leonard: No. No. I'm really tired now. Please. I couldn't
> square what I was doing with my honour if you like, my
> intelligence, if you like, my beliefs, if you like.

The sense of compromise which assailed him in the play's second act clearly became too much for him to bear. His actions receive a hostile response from Mrs Chater, who is upset because her boy had no opportunity to resign from active service before his death, but Leonard is unrepentant, challenging his family's approach to the situation they are facing: 'why are we unable to see ourselves now, anything, but in the rosy light we think of as shining on us before the war?' He is forceful in condemning the work of the Versailles treaty, and in doing so predicts prolonged trouble which will flow from what has been accomplished by 'the hurried nation making, the arbitrary drawing of borders. Treating Africa, as if it was ours to be disposed of, at will... So that it can only be time before some Mohamedan Cromwell will come surely, sooner or later.' He is bitter about the stymieing of the League of Nations, though hardly sides with America in his anger:

> Leonard: Countries have different reparations to make.
> Ours, if we had to make it, would be to do with empire
> and class. The American, I suppose, is different.
> Geoffrey: What's that?
> Leonard: Their expansion is based on the almost
> complete annihilation of their native people and on
> slavery. And the consequences of slavery, still hangs
> over them in a very tangible way. There is no doubt that
> they have the intention of subverting the British
> empire, to their own ends, when the time comes.

This prediction, of course, has the same effect as his invocation of a 'Mohamedan Cromwell' – it is a reminder to the audience that the moment they are watching was the beginning of the American century, as well as the beginning of a century of violence and upset in the Middle East. But this is not the centre of Leonard's anger, the reason he left his post. What enrages him above all is the way the Versailles treaty carved up the world in order to protect vested interests, to sustain the elite who brought about the carnage of the Great War:

> Leonard: In fact what we were doing in Paris can be described as an example of class action... Policy differences apart, and if the truth was told, we saw our own class interest as being best put to the service of a ruling class, just sophisticated enough to know how far it could go... And I thought I was working for the public good.

What he wishes for is some larger re-imagination of the social order, a redrawing of power relationships in society that might avoid future tragedy. He outlines the system as he sees it:

> Leonard: There is a large working class, with at one end of it an underclass, if you like, which if mobilised is unstoppable. And at the top, what you could call an aristocracy, if you like... it is unwise to ignore them, since they influence the rest.

This, he argues, is what the Versailles treaty should have tried to change; but 'we had forgotten the war in our effort to deal with the peace... and we are still in thrall to the system that brought it about.' The source of his despair is revealed to be the fact that the negotiators at the Astoria were simply not equal to the task of reimagining that system: 'it wasn't that my masters weren't doing what they thought was best. It was that the war was greater than the capacity and means they had to deal with the outcome. So it was forward to the status quo.' Leonard associates himself with these limited compromisers, recognising a revolutionary impulse in him which is held in check by his innate conservatism, a cause of caustic self-hatred:

> Leonard: Can there be liberty without equality, can there?
> Geoffrey: Not thinking of joining the Communist party, Leonard?

> Leonard: No, I'm not. Not that that makes me feel good
>   you know.
> Geoffrey: No.
> Leonard: Because Geoffrey, it means by implication, I will
>   be supporting you forever... I believe, really what
>   Constance believes, really. Freedom of the individual to
>   choose is it, Constance? Freedom to choose between
>   silk shirts.

Constance tries to move the conversation on, but Leonard has the last word with a grim prediction:

> Constance: All very interesting, but my concern is only
>   that we keep the peace...
> Leonard: The conflict at the heart of Europe is
>   unresolved. It is.

What Gill seeks to explore here is the reason for the failure of the Versailles treaty to do anything more than shore up the status quo. He locates that failure in the individual – in the fact that all decisions, even the very momentous, are made by individual men and women, and that on this occasion, the wrong people were round the table for anything imaginative to come from Versailles. They had been to the type of schools, and, as this play shows us, came from the type of households and families, which fettered their capacity to think their way into a better, more egalitarian social system. Leonard's dignity lies in the fact that he recognised this shortcoming and removed himself from the conversation, knowing he did not have the necessary will or imagination to create a new reality out of his work. Despite the suggestion from many around him that this is less heroic than staying at the Astoria and fighting to do what he could, Leonard does acquire a dignity in the play, a quality lent him by the play's closing scene, which favours Leonard's choice by allowing the last thing we see to be the last conversation he had with Gerald in 1914 before Gerald left for the war. What we are left with is an impression of all he has lost, all the grief that he has been weighed down by, all the anger which must inevitably have flowed from this. This

cannot fail to elicit the sympathy of an audience for the character of Leonard, who we know has had so much taken away from
him. The play ends by stepping back several years, as Gerald
steps onto the stage in fatigues. The conversation, again, has a
poignant Chekhovian tone, as so much is left unspoken beneath
the surface of the two mens' speech:

> Gerald: Well.
> Leonard: Yes.
> Gerald: I wanted to say goodbye.
> Leonard: Yes.
> Gerald: Thank you for your note.
> Leonard: Are you going this morning?
> Gerald: Yes. Now.
> Leonard: Oh.
> Gerald: I wondered if you wanted to come to the station
>   with me Leonard?
> Leonard: Yes of course.

The last thing we hear from Gerald, who we know will be
killed in the coming years, is his forced optimism for the future:

> Leonard: How are you feeling about it?
> Gerald: Looking forward. You know, apprehensive but,
>   you know, excited. I'm looking forward.

The last thing we see after Gerald and Leonard go out to walk
to the train station is the women left alone on stage, just as the
play began, and crying for the men who have been taken away
from them.

Gill's play revolves around vast ideas – the colossal import of
the Versailles conference, the inevitable failure of the western elite
to re-imagine itself into irrelevance, the extent to which the
imagination is the only limit to what is achievable in the world,
the way decisions or documents can shape a century of events –
but its heart lies in the telling of a human story, about loves and
lives abruptly terminated, the damage done to people by
violence, and the disabling effects of that damage on the

survivors who must live on without their loved ones. The shape
of the play leads us into a more intimate reading of the import of
Versailles than a writer less committed to a humanist view of life
might have pursued, funnelling us back into the personal and
domestic sphere having shown us the big world in Paris; it
focuses on relationships that have broken down, that cannot
grow, that cannot live in the aftermath of war. It is through analysis at the level of the individual life, not of the idea as an abstract,
that Gill's play accesses what is moving and tragic about the
events he dramatises. This is the virtue of drama over the kind of
discourse practised at the treaty negotiations surrounding the
Versailles conference. Drama is the place where those arguments
which are irresolvable can be fruitfully interrogated, presented
and circled, in a way that is impossible over a negotiating table. It
does this by analysing all stories through their impact on human
lives, at the level of the individual. Gill might not thank me for
using this soap box to defend any statement of Margaret
Thatcher's, but at a certain level, it is true that there is no such
thing as society. Just as there is no such thing, on one plane of
experience, the depictable experience of the world, as an idea.
You cannot put society or ideas on stage. What you can put on
stage are bodies, people, humans, lives. And you cannot resolve
grief through a treaty negotiation, but you can address its effect
on bodies and lives through theatre. Gill's focus on this human
plane allows us to read the pity and the tragedy of both war and
peace into his drama.

Versailles is a fascinating addition to Gill's work. In style, as a
play that happens largely in chronological order but folds back
into memory at its close, that takes place on a naturalistic set, that
is preoccupied with the unfulfillable relationship between two
young men, it can be seen as a natural companion to *The York
Realist*. But it is when the play is set against *Small Change* that a
more suggestive thematic continuity emerges. Mrs Harte states
in *Small Change*, 'the war finished me off. It was the start of
everything and it was the end of everything.' Though the war
hanging over *Versailles* is a different conflict, there could surely be
no more appropriate epigraph to the play than those words. I

have already noted that Leonard uses the past here to 'feel safe in its present moment', as Vincent puts it in *Small Change*; it should also be noted that the central, distinctive subject of Versailles, the treaty as a missed opportunity to re-imagine the world and dismantle the system that caused the war, is in fact an eloquent restatement of a dominant theme of *Small Change*, which is filled with Vincent's hypothetical scenarios for change: 'if we all put our shoulders to the wheel', and of a recurring theme throughout Gill's work, an ambivalent or hostile attitude towards 'taking part' in the social systems which enslave the people who, by enacting them, perpetuate their influence on our lives. By setting his drama among characters from the social background which dominates *Versailles*, and setting his play at a time where his characters have an opportunity to discuss this ambivalence at length, Gill is able to give new weight and consideration to this particular aspect of his subconscious. But it is nonetheless a continuation of a preoccupation which has existed throughout his work, underscoring his writing from that first extraordinary image in *The Sleepers Den*, the three women in bed together, and Mrs Shannon shutting out the world.

What struck me particularly after reading *Versailles* was the way it challenged me to slightly reimagine my idea of Gill's subject throughout his career. I had never particularly imagined Gill as a war writer; but this play, which put war and its impact centre-stage, drew out parallels across his work, in the dwelling on the war in *Cardiff East* and *Small Change*, in the memories of *Lovely Evening*, where Gill's subject had been the way communities or individuals, and by implication the societies around them, had been affected by war. By turning his attention to a different conflict, Gill highlighted for me his lasting preoccupation with the Second World War, during which he first grew into the world, and so during which many of his own first reference points were set. Gill's work is all about where he has come from, and his reading of the world is perhaps that we are the sum of our rememberings, and so it is no surprise that he might have drama-tised, throughout his career, the world that flowed from the conflict in whose shadow he began his own life. Here in *Versailles*, though, he has expanded his thinking, and become a writer whose subjects include the nature of trauma, the nature of grief, the way wars bring people together and pull people apart. Again, it is perhaps no surprise that these subjects preoccupy him. Gill's work is a sustained reading of the world around him, after all, and a response to the world he has lived in, and the century where he has spent most of his life was undoubtedly a story about the Great War and the impact of the Versailles treaty.

EPILOGUE

Allow me to end with an anecdote.

Some time shortly after the end of the First World War, the newspaper magnate William Randolph Hearst set up house with the actress Marion Davies in California. This caused the separation of Hearst from his wife Millicent (a former chorus girl fifteen years older than Davies), though they remained legally married until the end of Hearst's life.

Millicent Hearst lived in New York and became a major philanthropist of the period; however, she never did much for Herman Mankiewicz, who, at about the same time as Hearst was losing her husband to another woman, lost the most treasured possession of his childhood when he left his bicycle outside a New York library and came back out to find it had been taken. His parents, as punishment for losing the bicycle they had already bought him, refused to buy him another. Whether Millicent Hearst would have bought him a new one if she had heard his story of youthful heartbreak, we cannot know.

Twenty years later, shortly after the outbreak of the Second World War, Mankiewicz, who had become a writer, co-wrote a film about ambition, of which Hearst did everything he could to prevent the release. The film was *Citizen Kane*, and its central character was a not too heavily veiled portrait of Hearst. Mankiewicz came up with the film's main instigating plot device, and its opening line. As Kane died at the film's outset (it would then scroll back through time, like *The York Realist*, to show us how Kane got to that moment), he uttered a single last word: 'rosebud'. The search for the meaning of that word became the plot of the film. One of the reasons Hearst was particularly anxious to stop the film being distributed was that, according to Gore Vidal, who has it on good authority from a nephew of Hearst's, 'rosebud' was Hearst's nickname for Marion Davies's clitoris. How Mankiewicz might have known this, we cannot know.

The 'rosebud' in the screenplay is not, however, Marion Davies's clitoris: it far more closely resembles Mankiewicz's bicycle. We meet Rosebud very early in the story when it scrolls back to show us Kane's life. In the first scene from Kane's life depicted, the young Charles Foster Kane uses Rosebud to assault the man who takes him away from his home and his family and brings him to the city. Rosebud is, in fact, a sled, an image of childhood happiness from before Kane was taken away from his home, of a perfect time he reveals, at the end of his life, to have held in his mind throughout all the years of his success as what he loved most. In the film's closing sequence, the sled is burned as the investigators trying to track this elusive Rosebud down give up and Kane's stately pleasure dome is cleared.

When I was conducting the interviews for this book, more than one of Gill's closest and oldest collaborators said the word 'rosebud' to me. They thought of Gill's work as a puzzle whose source I might try and get back to through an investigation such as this. They couldn't have known quite what a chord they were sounding, because I have always had a fascination with Rosebud. Charles Foster Kane is played by two actors in *Citizen Kane*: Orson Welles, the film's director and co-writer with Mankiewicz, and Buddy Swann, who also appeared in *The Fighting Sullivans*, *The Ape*, *Scared Stiff* and various other films as a child actor before giving up the business as an adult. Buddy Swann has always transfixed me, for the simple reason that when we were eight years old we looked exactly alike. My own fascination with my past is complicatedly entangled with the face of that boy in that film, and so I read Gill's plays delighted that these two preoccupations might have somehow coagulated into one story, and entertained by the conception of this body of work as puzzle.

The clue these colleagues of Gill's were offering me was different to the one in the film. It's not hard to work out what Rosebud is in Gill's work – it is the past, the vanished world he continually revisits, and the emotional experience of memory (which is what it is for Kane as well). The clue lay in the fact that more than one of them invoked the film at all: Gill's contemporaries recognised his work as that of a man holding on to a memory of the past and his youth that was set above all subsequent experience as the source and centre of his life. At the conclusion of this study, I have one more metaphor to offer for the way Gill's plays might be read: as the visions of a man staring into a snowglobe, stoking the life in him with memories of the life he has passed through. As the questions of the private investigator trying to track down Rosebud. As Orson Welles wishing he could be Buddy Swann again.

What I have been documenting here is the heroic project of a man who, over fifty years, has stared at life and offered up the findings of his study. His achievement is, in part, a melancholy one, because his subject has continually been the enumeration of what he has lost, what he cannot live again. The plays are pursuits after rosebuds – snowglobes like Kane's which show him the world he loves but do not let him in. His achievement is also a beautiful one, because, as is the case with all writing, his project has been to cup his hands, catch his life as it flows through him and past him, and love his life as he holds it and examines it through the ironising lens of a play. Observed life performs differently to life when no one is looking at it: in poetic realism, the real acts of ordinary people become ritual as well, become meaningful and beautiful. So he has been able to give beauty to people's ordinary days.

It is this aspect of Gill's achievement that makes his work ultimately so important to my mind. When I first read Peter Gill, what spoke to me most strongly was the struggle his characters were involved in to express themselves, to find the words that could explain them and what it felt like to be them. Gerard's ineloquence in *Small Change* was, and remains for me, the centre of his work, the piece of writing for which I am most grateful, and the key to who Gill is as a writer. What he has always done in his theatre is try to reveal to us the currents of extraordinary, deep and powerful feeling that are always running beneath the surfaces of everyone: through loving attention, to reveal the love within every person in his work that motivates and explains them.

I began this book by writing at some length about a poet who has not featured frequently in the subsequent pages, but I return to Bernard O'Donoghue now. O'Donoghue and Gill have always been involved in the same project – the accessing of deep emotion through close attention to ordinary things, because just as our emotional lives are lost among visions of rissoles and bowls of porridge, so it is through looking hard at those everyday things that we see through to the life coursing beneath. This is how things can be made to last; this is why you number the stones. It will become the incantatory sounding into being of the emotions of a life, which are so often invisible to us in other people on an ordinary day.

I have one more poet to invoke – another man who has featured intermittently in these pages without yet taking the limelight, who Gill claims a more distant relationship with than I would ascribe to them. This is where Rosebud is most beautifully revealed and detailed, and so it is where I will end. If there is a secret Gill's plays has sought to reveal, it is the secret life recorded in John Donne's poem 'The Ecstasie', a study of those same hidden currents within human beings that are the subject of the theatre of Peter Gill.

> WHERE, like a pillow on a bed,
>   A pregnant bank swell'd up, to rest
> The violet's reclining head,
>   Sat we two, one another's best.
>
> Our hands were firmly cemented
>   By a fast balm, which thence did spring ;
> Our eye-beams twisted, and did thread
>   Our eyes upon one double string.
>
> So to engraft our hands, as yet
>   Was all the means to make us one;
> And pictures in our eyes to get
>   Was all our propagation.

As, 'twixt two equal armies, Fate
    Suspends uncertain victory,
Our souls – which to advance their state,
    Were gone out – hung 'twixt her and me.

And whilst our souls negotiate there,
    We like sepulchral statues lay;
All day, the same our postures were,
    And we said nothing, all the day.

If any, so by love refined,
    That he soul's language understood,
And by good love were grown all mind,
    Within convenient distance stood,

He – though he knew not which soul spake,
    Because both meant, both spake the same –
Might thence a new concoction take,
    And part far purer than he came.

This ecstasy doth unperplex
    (We said) and tell us what we love;
We see by this, it was not sex;
    We see, we saw not, what did move:

But as all several souls contain
    Mixture of things they know not what,
Love these mix'd souls doth mix again,
    And makes both one, each this, and that.

A single violet transplant,
    The strength, the colour, and the size –
All which before was poor and scant –
    Redoubles still, and multiplies.

When love with one another so
    Interanimates two souls,
That abler soul, which thence doth flow,
    Defects of loneliness controls.

We then, who are this new soul, know,
    Of what we are composed, and made,
For th' atomies of which we grow
    Are souls, whom no change can invade.

But, O alas! so long, so far,
    Our bodies why do we forbear?
They are ours, though not we; we are
    Th' intelligences, they the spheres.

We owe them thanks, because they thus
    Did us, to us, at first convey,
Yielded their senses' force to us,
    Nor are dross to us, but allay.

On man heaven's influence works not so,
    But that it first imprints the air;
For soul into the soul may flow,
    Though it to body first repair.

As our blood labours to beget
    Spirits, as like souls as it can;
Because such fingers need to knit
    That subtle knot, which makes us man;

So must pure lovers' souls descend
    To affections, and to faculties,
Which sense may reach and apprehend,
    Else a great prince in prison lies.

To our bodies turn we then, that so
    Weak men on love reveal'd may look;
Love's mysteries in souls do grow,
    But yet the body is his book.

And if some lover, such as we,
    Have heard this dialogue of one,
Let him still mark us, he shall see
    Small change when we're to bodies gone.

APPENDIX I
PRODUCTION HISTORY

1965

A Collier's Friday Night	D.H. Lawrence	Royal Court Theatre
The Sleepers Den★	Peter Gill	Royal Court Theatre
Who'll Save the Ploughboy?	Frank.D. Gilroy	Nederlands Kamertoneel

1966

The Local Stigmatic	Heathcote Williams	Royal Court Theatre
The Ruffian on the Stair	Joe Orton	Royal Court Theatre
A Provincial Life	Anton Chekhov, adap. Peter Gill	Royal Court Theatre
The Dwarfs	Harold Pinter	Traverse Theatre, Edinburgh
The Local Stigmatic	Heathcote Williams	Traverse Theatre, Edinburgh
O'Flaherty VC	G.B. Shaw	Mermaid Theatre

1967

The Soldier's Fortune	Thomas Otway	Royal Court Theatre
O'Flaherty VC	G.B. Shaw	Vancouver Festival
Crimes of Passion	Joe Orton	Royal Court Theatre
The Daughter-in-Law	D.H. Lawrence	Royal Court Theatre

1968

The Daughter-in-Law	D.H. Lawrence	Royal Court Theatre
A Collier's Friday Night	D.H. Lawrence	Royal Court Theatre
The Widowing of Mrs Holroyd	D.H. Lawrence	Royal Court Theatre

1969

Life Price	Jeremy Seabrook & Michael O'Neill	Royal Court Theatre
Over Gardens Out	Peter Gill	Royal Court Theatre
The Sleepers Den	Peter Gill	Royal Court Theatre
Much Ado About Nothing	Shakespeare	Stratford, Conn.

1970
| *Hedda Gabler* | Henrik Ibsen | Stratford, Ontario |
| *Landscape and Silence* | Harold Pinter | Lincoln Center, New York |

1971
| *The Duchess of Malfi* | John Webster | Royal Court Theatre |
| *Macbeth* | Shakespeare | Stratford, Ontario |

1972
Crete and Sergeant Pepper	John Antrobus	Royal Court Theatre
The Daughter-in-Law	D.H. Lawrence	Schauspielhaus, Bochum
A Midsummer Night's Dream	Shakespeare	Schauspielhaus, Zurich

1973
| *The Merry-Go-Round* | D.H. Lawrence, adap. Peter Gill | Royal Court Theatre |

1974
| *Twelfth Night* | Shakespeare | RSC |

1975
The Fool	Edward Bond	Royal Court Theatre
Fishing	Michael Weller	Public Theater New York
As You Like It	Shakespeare	Nottingham Playhouse

1976
| *Small Change* | Peter Gill | Royal Court Theatre |

1977
| *Small Change* | Peter Gill | Riverside Studios |

1978
| *The Cherry Orchard* | Anton Chekhov | Riverside Studios |
| *The Changeling* | Thomas Middleton & William Rowley | Riverside Studios |

1979
| *Measure for Measure* | Shakespeare | Riverside Studios |

1980
| *Julius Caesar* | Shakespeare | Riverside Studios |
| *Scrape off the Black* | Tunde Ikoli | Riverside Studios |

1981

A Month In The Country	Ivan Turgenev, trans. Isaiah Berlin	National Theatre
Don Juan	Moliere, trans. John Fowles	National Theatre
Much Ado About Nothing	Shakespeare	National Theatre

1982

Danton's Death	Georg Buchner, adap. Howard Brenton	National Theatre
Major Barbara	G.B. Shaw	National Theatre

1983

Tales from Hollywood	Christopher Hampton	National Theatre
Small Change	Peter Gill	National Theatre
Kick for Touch	Peter Gill	National Theatre

1984

Antigone	Sophocles, trans. C.A. Trypanis	National Theatre
Venice Preserv'd	Thomas Otway	National Theatre
Fool for Love	Sam Shepard	National Theatre

1985

The Murderers	Daniel Mornin	National Theatre
Fool for Love	Sam Shepard	Lyric Theatre, Shaftesbury Ave
As I Lay Dying	William Faulkner, adap. Peter Gill	National Theatre
A Twist of Lemon	Alex Renton	National Theatre
In The Blue	Peter Gill	National Theatre
Bouncing	Rosemary Wilton	National Theatre
Up For None	Mick Mahoney	National Theatre
The Garden of England	Peter Cox	National Theatre

1987

Mean Tears	Peter Gill	National Theatre
Bow Down, Down By The Greenwood Side	Harrison Birtwhistle	Queen Elizabeth Hall
The Marriage of Figaro	W.A. Mozart	Opera North

1988

Mrs Klein	Nicholas Wright	National Theatre

1989

Juno and the Paycock	Sean O'Casey	National Theatre

1992
The Way of the World   William Congreve   Lyric Hammersmith

1994
New England   Richard Nelson   RSC

1995
A Patriot for Me   John Osborne   RSC
Uncle Vanya   Anton Chekhov,   Field Day
                               trans. Frank McGuinness

1997
Cardiff East   Peter Gill   National Theatre
Tongue of a Bird   Ellen Mclaughlin   Almeida Theatre

1999
Certain Young Men   Peter Gill   Almeida Theatre
Friendly Fire   Peter Gill   NT Connections

2000
Speed-the-Plow   David Mamet   New Ambassadors
                                                   Theatre

The Seagull   Anton Chekhov,
                               adap. Peter Gill   RSC

2001
Luther   John Osborne   National Theatre
The Look Across The Eyes   Peter Gill   BBC Radio
and *Lovely Evening*
The York Realist   Peter Gill   English Touring Theatre/
                                                   Royal Court Theatre

2002
Original Sin   Peter Gill   Sheffield Crucible
Small Change   Peter Gill★   Sheffield Crucible
Kick for Touch   Peter Gill★   Sheffield Crucible
Mean Tears   Peter Gill★   Sheffield Crucible
Friendly Fire   Peter Gill★   Sheffield Crucible

2003
Scenes from the Big Picture Owen McCafferty   Donmar Warehouse

2004
Romeo and Juliet   Shakespeare   RSC

2005
Days of Wine and Roses   J.P. Miller   Donmar Warehouse

	&Owen McCafferty	
Epitaph for George Dillon	John Osborne	Comedy Theatre
	& Anthony Creighton	

2006

The Voysey Inheritance	H. Granville-Barker	National Theatre
Look Back In Anger	John Osborne	Theatre Royal Bath

2007

Gaslight	Patrick Hamilton	Old Vic
The Importance of Being Earnest	Oscar Wilde	Theatre Royal Bath

2008

Small Change	Peter Gill	Donmar Warehouse

2009

Another Door Closed	Peter Gill	Theatre Royal Bath

2010

The Aliens	Annie Baker	Bush Theatre

2011

66 Books	Caroline Bird	Bush Theatre

2012

A Provincial Life	Anton Chekhov, adap. Peter Gill	National Theatre Wales
Making Noise Quietly	Robert Holman	Donmar Warehouse
Sergeant Musgrave's Dance	John Arden**	Royal Court Theatre

2014

Versailles	Peter Gill	Donmar Warehouse

* Production not directed by Gill.
** Rehearsed reading.

Appendix 2
Works by Peter Gill

Plays
Plays 1 – The Sleepers Den, Over Gardens Out, Small Change, Kick for Touch, In the Blue, Mean Tears (London: Faber and Faber, 2002)
Plays 2 – Cardiff East, Certain Young Men, The York Realist, Original Sin, The Look Across the Eyes, Lovely Evening (London: Faber and Faber, 2008)
Another Door Closed (London: Faber and Faber, 2011)
Versailles (London: Faber and Faber, 2014)

Adaptations
The Cherry Orchard (London: Oberon Books, 1995)
The Seagull (London: Oberon Books, 2000)
A Provincial Life (London: Faber and Faber, 2012)

Memoir
Apprenticeship (London: Oberon Books, 2008)

INDEX